Latter Rain

The Final

Outpouring

Dr. Tomeka Wooten

ISBN- 979-8-9865839-4-5

House of Stone Publishing – Macon, Georgia

Latter Rain

The Final

Outpouring

Contents

Acknowledgements 6

Introduction.. 9

The Seven Churches.. 15

The Backslidden Church 19

The Persecuted Church.. 21

The Compromising Church 23

The Corrupted Church... 27

The Dying Church... 29

The Faithful Church 31

The Lukewarm Church.. 33

Valleys 37

The Valley of Elah 39

The Valley of the Shadow of Death 41

The Valley of Baca... 43

The Valley of Achor.. 47

The Valley of Berachah 51

The God of the Valleys.. 55

What the Enemy Meant for Bad 59

No Weapon Formed 61

Seeds.. 65

The Fruit of the Spirit.. 73

Love.. 77

Joy 79

Peace 83

Patience 85

Gentleness 87

Goodness 89

Faithfulness 93

Meekness 95

Temperance 97

Seasons 103

The Former and Latter Rain 107

The Prophet and the Prostitute 111

The Maturation of Christ in the Saints 113

The Last Great Outpouring 115

Conclusion 119

About the Author 125

Acknowledgements

To my great grandmother (The late Mother/Evangelist, Ida Catherine Dennis) thank you for laying the spiritual foundations for this family. Thank you for all your prayers which are now manifesting. You would be so proud. Thank you for always being a great example of a woman of God and for teaching me the true meaning of holiness! The prayers of the righteous availeth much!

To my husband Chris, thank you for always being supportive even when you didn't understand and for loving me unconditionally for who I am and who God has called me to be!

To my children; my eldest son, Christopher Jr., my youngest son, Caleb, and my grandson, Caio. Thank you for loving me and allowing me to be who God has called me to be. Which is first and foremost a mother to you all. My home is my first ministry. I know I didn't always get it right, but thank you for loving me despite of. You have brought so much joy and inspiration into my life.

To my mother, thank you for the tough love that reminds me daily of who I am, for always believing in me and pushing me to my greatest potential. You never let me settle. Thanks for picking me up when I was down in spirit, for all your wisdom, encouragement and for being not just my mother, but my first mentor and friend. Most of all thank you for teaching me how to war in the spirit and how to be a mighty woman of God!

To Bishop Michael Burney and Pastor Alice Burney, thank you for taking me into the Living Waters Full Gospel family, for loving me and always being willing to pray for me and my family. Thanks for giving me such an anointed, foundational teaching, showing me what a godly marriage looks like and for all of your genuine love and kindness. Thank you for being there as my spiritual parents.

Thank you to my leaders Apostle Nora Jackson and Pastor Carrie Works, for accepting me into the Global Church Family. You help me stretch to that next level in God. Thank you for the prophetic, apostolic teaching and kingdom building that has helped usher me right where I'm supposed to be.

Thanks to Dr. Aaron Hamilton and Elder Sheila Hamilton for pouring into me with so much love and kindness and for seeing in me what I didn't see in myself. Thank you for providing a judgment free zone to grow and push past my insecurities and fears. You helped me to heal and pushed me to my greatest potential. You encouraged me not to give up and stick with God no matter what. Thanks for always encouraging me to walk in my calling and for being great mentors; such a great man and woman of God.

Thanks to my prayer partners, a host of family and friends that supported me and kept me lifted. You know who you are. Those that have been there for me in my most vulnerable moments. Thanks for a listening ear, encouragement, advice and most of all, thanks for your prayers.

To my father, Radford Williams, thank you for loving me, teaching me all that you know, being a listening ear and for your encouragement.

Lastly, thank You Heavenly Father for the gifts and anointing that You have placed down on the inside of me. Proverbs 18:16 "A man's gift makes room for him" (NKJV). May I continue to be a humble, willing vessel, fulfilling the purpose that God has for me and that He be glorified in Heaven.

Introduction

On the seventh day of fasting, I arose from my sleep and heard the words "Latter Rain." I heard it spoken three times; with each time the voice was louder and more intense than the last. Then I heard the voice of the Lord say, "Some have prayed, fasted, cried and sown seeds righteously and I'm about to rain down on my people." I do believe that this was a prophetic message given to me from the Lord. Over the next few days, I began to seek the Lord for more revelation and understanding regarding what I heard. As I sought the Lord, He began to pour into me regarding His message and it's relevance for such a time as this. I decided to write this book about the final outpouring of the Holy Spirit; relating to what God wants His people to know and hold on to during this time. Our life experiences can draw us closer to Christ, ultimately bringing us into the full maturation of Christ in us (the Saints). In this book, I want to reflect on where we have been compared to where we are now in Christ. I wrote this book for the encouragement of the Saints, that repentance and refocus on God takes place. This book will give some prophetic insight and foresight on what's to come, so that we may be well prepared and ready for the return of Christ.

God wants His children to remain prayerful, hopeful and not lose faith. He wants to remind us that He is near and always speaking throughout scriptures, dreams, visions and even nature. According to Acts 2:17 (KJV) it states "And it shall come to pass in the last days, saith God, I will pour out of my Spirit upon all flesh: and your sons and your daughters shall prophesy, and your young men shall see visions, and your old men shall dream dreams:" A tremendous revival is on the way. This upcoming revival is the progress of the gospel of the kingdom at hand that will be preached to all the nations. Although this is biblical, I believe in my spirit that the latter-rain outpouring is connected to the revival spoken of in the scriptures. Before this revival takes place, there are some things that must precede this revival. During the end times, a great apostasy also called the "falling away" is nothing more than mere rebellion, rejection and abandonment of the truth. This is happening now.

God said the wheat and the tare will grow up together until harvest time. The separating of the wheat from the tare is necessary as He is only returning for His church; a church without spot or wrinkle. Likened to a bride adorned for her groom on that special wedding day. God is perfecting Himself within the church. This revival will also be accompanied by a reformation which must take place. You cannot have one without the other. The revival signifies a renewal of spiritual life. A quickening of the powers of mind, heart and a resurrection from spiritual death. Reformation signifies a change in ideas, theories, habits and practices. Reformation will not bring forth the fruit of righteousness unless it's connected to the revival of the Spirit. Revival and reformation are to do their appointed work, and in doing this work they must blend. *(RH Feb. 25, 1902)* *(https://www.ellenwhitedefend.com/Books-EGW/lde/lde13.htm, n.d.)* Time out for traditions. God wants the church to get back to the basics. There must be change because this outpouring can't take place without it. The final outpouring is for the renewal of the church that believers walk in Godliness. This has not been witnessed since apostolic times.

There have been other sicknesses, diseases, outbreaks and pandemics. However, the Covid-19 pandemic has affected our everyday life. It has adversely affected the global economy and it feels apocalyptic. There's a shifting taking place in the spiritual realm which is affecting humanity. This is a time of great uncertainty. We have been pushed beyond our comfort zones. We have been challenged with new technological ways of teaching, learning, doing business and serving God. Some may say the church has left the building since COVID-19. Before the pandemic, in my opinion, church attendance had been declining for years. There had been a growing weariness with the way we did church long before the pandemic. Based on Barna Research, *"Surprisingly, even 57% of church-going adults said they were tired or somewhat tired of the usual church experience." "Note: This is from the people who were still attending church. This crisis has been an identified accelerator and now that the pandemic has stretched on for months, the habits people have formed will likely become even more permanent in the post-pandemic era. Regular attenders may become less regular. Irregular attenders may become even less frequent attenders. In this cultural moment, that is not necessarily a sign of decreasing devotion. It's just a sign of a shifting culture."* *(https://careynieuwhof.com/the-church-has-left-the-building-5-*

truths-about-future-church-attendance-and-commitment/),   *n.d.)*

The enemy's plan was to keep the churches closed so that no one would attend. In my opinion, those truly seeking after God were drawn closer to Him. People slowly but surely are beginning to realize and understand that we are the church. It is about your personal relationship with Him and your desire to know Him. Many have experienced sickness, unemployment, death of loved ones and suffered great loss. Depression and suicide is at an all-time high.

One thing I know is that this pandemic has changed the way we do things. People have had to adapt. Virtual services allow us to travel all around the world. Leaders can minister every day of the week, verses one or two days a week. We must not despise change. If we embrace it and give thanks in all things, God can do more with us. Through our trials and tribulations, God is reconciling His people back to Him. We must understand that He is in control. We must not lean to our own understanding. We must simply trust Him and pray. God has a plan. We must not make the mistake of thinking just because someone is not attending services in person they are not engaging. Jesus didn't say, "Attend me.' He said, 'Follow me."

It has never been about the number of people in attendance but more about the equipping of the people for the coming of Christ. God is raising up warriors that walk in holiness and are seeking a personal relationship with Him. They are being taught how to fight by using the authority and power that He has given. It is important in our commission as believers that we assist in providing an environment that fosters spiritual growth and maturity. Time is up for the traditional and familiar things that so many Saints are used to. God is doing a new thing in the earth realm. We must be in alignment and on one accord so that we do not miss the mark. According to 2 Thessalonians 2:1-3 (KJV) it states, *"Now we beseech you, brethren, by the coming of our Lord Jesus Christ, and by our gathering together unto him, 2 That ye be not soon shaken in mind, or be troubled, neither by spirit, nor by word, nor by letter as from us, as that the day of Christ is at hand. 3 Let no man deceive you by any means: for that day shall not come, except there comes a falling away first, and that man of sin be revealed, the son of perdition."*

Now that we know there must be a falling away first, we as men and women of God, must understand that we are in a seasonal, spiritual, paradigm shift. Our salvation depends on us being in an unwavering position. We do not compromise the gospel. We must be open to adapt to the changing times. The mission is and should always remain the same; winning souls for Christ. It is God's will that everyone repents and is saved. He has equipped the men and women of God that they may be used by Him, for His glory. He wants to reclaim every backslider, stir up the lukewarm and draw unbelievers to His son Jesus Christ; so that they may also be saved. This is not the time to become fearful, go into hiding and retreat. Through Christ, we are already victorious. We must fight with faith for our salvation like never before. How do we do this? We must make sure that we are in right relationship with God. How do we get in right relationship with God? Jesus Christ provides the way. We first recognize our condition; we believe, repent and receive Christ. We pray, seek Him, abide in His presence, study His word, obey Him and trust Him by having faith.

As Christians we must understand that we are the church. The church is in us. We may gather in our homes, in small groups and in the community. By doing so we will make an impact in the world. Most importantly, we must not lose our faith, our passion and zeal for what God has called us to do. To some, the church may have left the physical building. However, in a season such as this, we must stay encouraged and trust that God's hand is all over it. He is moving amongst the earth like never before. The purpose of this book is to also identify the plan and promises of God. Providing hope for believers that they may remain encouraged and strengthened through His word at all times. In this book, I will identify the condition of the body of Christ during this era. I will elaborate on biblical prophecy by unveiling what has led us to where we are now as a nation. I will unveil divine revelation that God wants us to know regarding the things which are and the things that will surely come to pass. I will identify the churches of that time in comparison with the churches of today. God is always speaking but the question is, are we listening?

The Seven Churches

John was in the Spirit on the Lord's Day and heard God speak to him. He instructed him to write a book and send it to the Seven Churches of Asia Minor. They are the churches of Ephesus, Smyrna, Pergamos, Thyatira, Sardis, Philadelphia and Laodicea. When John received this message he was a prisoner on the Isle of Patmos. He heard behind him a "great voice," as of a trumpet and when he turned he saw "Seven Golden Candlesticks." Standing in their midst was one like unto the "Son of Man," who held in His right hand Seven Stars. He was told that the Seven Stars were the Angels which represented the ministers or messengers of the Seven Churches. The Seven Candlesticks represent the Seven Churches. A candlestick requires a lighted wick which is self-consuming. A lamp stand is simply a holder for a lamp whose light feeds from a reservoir of oil. Typifying and representing the oil of the Holy Spirit. Christ does not look upon the churches as the light, but simply the light holder. John's attention was called to the condition of these churches. These Seven Churches were representatives of churches chosen with certain characteristics. These characteristics were typical of the Church of Christ from the end of the first century down to the time of Christ's return. The messages of Christ to these seven churches of Asia Minor are mentioned in the book of Revelation 1:10-13.

The letters to the Seven Churches can be understood as

advice and warnings throughout all ages. Jesus Himself is giving the commendations and rebukes. Written by Apostle John, "who was the last remaining disciple, aged, banished on the isle of Patmos, whom God used to pen this last great book." (Cook, 2006)

"The Seven Churches of Revelation 2 and 3 were congregations of the Church of God in the first century. Located in Asia Minor (now modern Turkey), these churches represented actual communities of early Christians; not buildings or meeting halls. In addressing each of these congregations, God said that He knew their works. Knowing the challenges they were facing and how they were responding, He admonished them to repent of their mistakes and to remain faithful in order to receive salvation. Although their circumstances varied, this message was similar for each church." *The seven congregations were intended to encourage the members in these cities to hold fast to God's way of life so they could be rewarded in the future."* (Treybig, 2018) The Seven Churches were formed around 50 AD. *"The order of the messages to the churches seems to be divinely selected to give prophetically the main movement of church history."* (Walvoord, 1989) This interpretation of the "Messages to the Seven Churches" was hidden to the early church as time was required for church history to develop and be written. A comparison could have been made to reveal the correspondence, only if it had been known that the Seven Churches stood for seven church periods; that would have to elapse before Christ could return. The character of these Seven Churches is descriptive of the church during seven periods of her history. The distinctive conditions of those churches are not to be forgotten as they were in the exact condition in John's day.

We see that at the close of the first century, the leaven of false doctrine was at work in the churches. The churches are named in order because of the peculiar characteristic of each church; apply to the period of church history to which it is assigned. The churches were named in order to reflect the peculiar characteristics of the church at that time in history.

It must not be forgotten that these are distinctive characteristics of each church period and these traits do not disappear with that period. It continues down through the next period and so on until the end. Thus, increasing the imperfections of the visible church, until it ends in an open apostasy, as referenced in the corresponding link. *The Messages to the Seven Churches Compared with Church History."*

(https://www.blueletterbible.org/study/larkin/dt/22.cfm, 2018)

Dr. Tomeka Wooten

The Backslidden Church

Ephesus Revelation 2:1-7

Ephesus is the first of the Seven Churches. It was located in the city of Ephesus. Its name means desirable, darling, beloved and relaxation. Ephesus the city, was the home of the temple pagan goddess Diana; the goddess of ancient fertility. Ephesus was a wicked, yet prosperous city in the ancient world. It was believed to have had 250,000 people. Thousands would come to engage in pagan worship and practices. The character of the church during the Ephesians period is outlined during the church period from AD 70 to AD 170. This church was founded by Paul, continued by Timothy and pastored by John. Ephesus was also a church that labored tirelessly for the Lord. This church had a mission to touch a pagan city with the gospel. They placed priority on their work for Christ. They were faithful, committed and showed patience through endurance under trial. They were steadfast and unmovable in the midst of their circumstances. They were also a separated church that couldn't stand evil.

The problem with the church of Ephesus was that it lost its first love and became a backslidden church. It was so involved in its works; they forgot their love for Christ. Paul, the founder, warned the church of what would happen, in his parting message. "For I know this, that after my departing shall grievous wolves enter in among you, not sparing the flock. Also, of your own selves shall men arise, speaking perverse things, to draw away disciples after them." Acts 20:29-30. (KJV) The significance of this warning to Ephesus is seen in the commendation of the Message, verse 6 "But this thou hast, that thou hatest the deeds of the Nicolaitans which I also hate." Here, the wolves Paul were referring to were the Nicolaitanes. "They were a party in the church who were trying to establish a priestly order, perhaps trying to model the church after the Old Testament order. These were priests, Levites, and common people. Niko means to conquer, to overthrow and Laos means the people or laity. They were trying to establish a holy order of men and place them over the laity, which was foreign to the New Testament plan. They were not to be called pastors, but clergy, bishops, archbishops, cardinals and popes. This is where the dogma of "Apostolic Succession" and the separation of the clergy from the laity, a thing that God hates, originated. "The Church at Ephesus was not deceived, but recognized them as false apostles and liars." *(https://www.blueletterbible.org/study/larkin/dt/22.cfm, 2018)*

The Persecuted Church

Smyrna Revelation 2:8-11

Smyrna means bitterness but it also means Myrrh, which is an ointment associated with death. The church was named this because of the bitter persecution that they had endured. The meaning of the word Myrrh is a prophecy of the persecution and death which was to befall the members of the Smyrna Church. They were told not to fear the things that they should be called on to suffer, but to be faithful unto death; not until death. They were not to recant when called upon to face a Martyr's death but remain faithful until death which would relieve them of their suffering. Their reward would be a Crown of Life which is known as the Martyr's crown. They were told that the author of their long suffering would be the Devil. The duration was to be ten days, which was doubtless a prophetic reference to the Ten Great Persecutions under the Roman Emperors, beginning with Nero, AD 64 and ending with Diocletian in AD 310. "Seven of these "Great Persecutions" occurred during the "Smyrna Period" of Church History. It may also refer to the 10 years of the last and most fierce persecution under Diocletian. This period extended from AD 170 to Constantine AD 312." *(https://www.blueletterbible.org/study/larkin/dt/22.cfm, 2018)*

This church had been faithful standing for Christ, therefore they received no criticism from the Lord. Revelation 2:9 (KJV) states "9 I know thy works, and tribulation, and poverty, (but thou art rich) and I know the blasphemy of them which say they are Jews, and are not, but are the synagogue of Satan." (Nelson, 1982) Jesus is saying here that He is not just an outsider looking in. He has also been there. He identifies with the needs of the church and knows the tribulations (great economic and social pressures) and stresses. In verse 9 He was also talking about the criticism against them by the children of Satan. These were probably the Jews that tried to tear down the church reputation by criticizing and slandering their name. But this church was storing up riches that would never pass away; eternal riches invested in the kingdom of Heaven. According to Matthew 6:18-20 (KJV), "18 That thou appear not unto men to fast, but unto thy Father which is in secret: and thy Father, which seeth in secret, shall reward thee openly. 19 Lay not up for yourselves treasures upon earth, where moth and rust doth corrupt, and where thieves break through and steal: 20 But lay up for yourselves treasures in heaven, where neither moth nor rust doth corrupt, and where thieves do not break through nor steal." (Nelson, 1982) The Church at Smyrna had given their all and was promised a Crown of Life for their faithfulness. There was no condemnation found.

The Compromising Church

Pergamos Revelation 2:12-17

When Attalus III, the Priest King of the Chaldean Hierarchy, fled before the conquering Persians to Pergamos and settled there; Satan shifted his capital from Babylon to Pergamos. Pergamos was also called Satan's Seat. "Where Satan's throne is," refers to the fact that Satan ruled from Pergamum as it was the official center of emperor worship in Asia. Initially, he persecuted the followers of Christ. Antipas was one of the faithful martyrs that was persecuted. But soon Attalus changed his tactics from persecuting Christians and began to exalt the church. Constantine united the church and state and offered all kinds of inducements for worldly people to come into the church. Constantine's motive was more political than religious. He wished to merge the Christian and pagan subjects into one people and thus consolidate his empire. This resulted in a union in which two false and pernicious doctrines crept into the church. The first false doctrine was the Doctrine of Balaam and the second was the Doctrine of the Nicolaitans. This doctrine was previously considered and mentioned under the Message to the Church at Ephesus. The foothold it had secured in the church was seen in the first great council of the church held at Nicaea, in AD 325. This council was composed of about 1,500 delegates.

The laymen outnumbered the bishops 5 to 1. It was a council full of intrigue and political methods. From the supremacy of the clergy over the laity, it was evident that the Doctrine of the Nicolaitans had secured a strong and permanent foothold. Constantine brought the church and the Roman Empire together and married them. The church became married to the world at that point instead of married to Christ. Paganism began to merge with Christianity. Pagan temples became Christian churches. The pagan priest did not want to lose favor with Rome. They had been in Rome's favor all this time so they converted their temples into churches. They still worshipped the idols, but they just renamed them.

Therefore the same idol, the same statues, but had a different name. Lines were blurred and it became hard to distinguish the true Christians from those who just said they were. You could not tell them apart. The church and the world were indeed married. The Doctrine of Balaam is disclosed in the story of Balaam found in the Book of Numbers, chapters 22 to 25 inclusive. When the Children of Israel were on their way to Canaan and had reached the land of Moab, Balak the king of Moab sent for Balaam the Son of Beor to come and curse them. When the Lord would not permit Balaam to curse Israel, he suggested to Balak that he invite them to the licentious feasts of Baal Peor. Thus, causing Israel to fall into a snare that would anger the Lord; provoking Him to destroy them. This thing that Balak did caused the men of Israel to participate in sensual feasts. Seeing the daughters of Moab, they committed whoredoms with them, further kindling God's anger. Resulting in Him sending a plague that destroyed 42,000 of them. The word

Pergamos means marriage. When the church entered into a union with the state it was guilty of spiritual fornication or Balaamism. To the church of Pergamos, according to Revelation 2:16 (KJV), God is warning them to repent. "16 Repent; or else I will come unto thee quickly and will fight against them with the sword of my mouth." He is warning them to change their ways. God was not pleased with the compromising of the truth. Revelation 2:17 (KJV) states "17 He that hath an ear, let him hear what the Spirit saith unto the churches; To him that overcometh will I give to eat of the hidden manna, and will give him a white stone, and in the stone a new name written, which no man knoweth saving he that receiveth it." The reward that was promised was hidden manna which speaks of the truths of the word of God. He will replace false doctrine with true doctrine and feed the hungry soul; feasting from Him and what He has to offer. The white stone represents "Not Guilty." The white stone was given to a man that was acquitted in the court of law. He was declared not guilty. We have been justified and not guilty in God's eyes.

Dr. Tomeka Wooten

The Corrupted Church

Thyatira Revelation 2:18-29

Thyatira was the smallest of the seven cities in Asia Minor that Jesus gave his longest message to. Christ's commendation of this Church, lays the emphasis on their "works." Jesus establishes His identity. Verse 18 mentions His eyes were like unto a flame of fire, referring to His penetrating power. His feet were like brass referring to judgment. "He introduces Himself to the church establishing His identity and then speaks to Thyatira concerning their works. (Cook, 2006) "Jesus is the Son of God and wants us not to take His words lightly. Although they were loving, serving and faithful, they felt deserving of merit for their works of Supererogation. But He had a complaint to make against them. He charges them not merely with permitting a bad woman; Jezebel, who called herself a prophetess, to remain in the Church. But also permitted her to teach her pernicious doctrines, to seduce the servants to commit fornication and to eat things sacrificed to idols. Jesus likened her to the Old Testament Jezebel, which enticed Israel to worship Baal.

Jezebel was teaching the church to compromise with the religion of Rome to receive favor, rather than to stand with Christ. Jesus was angered and offended that they put up with people in the church that did not believe in the truth. He came and died so that we might know the truth. He gave Jezebel a chance to repent but she did not. Jezebel typified a system likened unto the Papal Church. The Papal Church introduced images and pictures into its churches for the people to bow down and idolize. It claims that the teaching of the church is superior to the Word of God. The study of the Papal System was from AD 606 to the Reformation AD 1520. Its institution of the "Sacrifice of the Mass" and other Pagan rites, reveals in it the sway of "Jezebelism." It was a period of "Jezebelistic Persecution," as seen in the wars of the Crusades and the rise of the Inquisition.

Today, there are many people that fumble their chances of being saved because of procrastination and refusing to come to repentance. Revelation 2:23 (KJV) speaks about the reward of the wicked. They will be judged according to their works. There is also a reward for the righteous. There were some that did not bend or fold and remained clean; not tolerating the wicked teachings of Jezebel. Unto them he speaks and said in Revelation 2:24-28 (KJV) "24 Now to you I say, and[a] to the rest in Thyatira, as many as do not have this doctrine, who have not known the depths of Satan, as they say, I will[b] put on you no other burden. 25 But hold fast what you have till I come. 26 And he who overcomes, and keeps My works until the end, to him I will give power over the nations—27 'He shall rule them with a rod of iron; They shall be dashed to pieces like the potter's vessels'[c]—as I also have received from My Father; 28 and I will give him the morning star." Revelation 2:24-28 (Nelson, 1982)

 The Dying Church

Sardis Revelation 3:1-5

This church was referred to as the greatest in Asia Minor with a great reputation. It was a city of the past that had lost its greatness living off its formal reputation. Jesus said He knew three things about them: "I know thou works", "I know thou hast a name that thou livest" and lastly "I know thou art dead." Jesus is saying "you are deaf because you have forsaken the purpose for which you were created." They were dying because they had not endured the Holy Spirit and didn't share the gospel with the lost. The first sign of spiritual rigor mortis is when a church stops winning the lost. Christians should lead people to Christ.

Sardis had become accustomed to their blessings and comfortable in worship. God encouraged them to hold fast, repent and get back to work. They were spiritually sleep and had become complacent. Sardis, the Dead or Dying Church was a formalistic church. It had a form of Godliness but without the power. The meaning of the word Sardis is "the escaping one" or "those who come out," making it an excellent type of the church of the Reformation Period. This period began about AD 1500 when Martin Luther and other reformers protested against the false teaching, tyranny and claims of the Papal Church. The condition of affairs in the realm dominated by the Papal Church became intolerable and came to a crisis when Martin Luther on October 31,

1517 AD approached the door of the Castle Church in Wittenberg, Germany and nailed a piece of paper to it containing the 95 revolutionary opinions that would begin the Protestant Reformation. When reformation set in, it was more of a struggle for political liberty than it was for a pure Christian or religious movement.

The Sardis Period extended from AD 1520 to about AD 1750. For those that were still faithful, Jesus promised them that they would be robed in white; meaning they would stand before God clean without the blood of the lost on their garments. Their name would not be blotted out of the Book of Life. The message to those who are asleep in Sardis, is to awake and repent. To those that are faithful, the message is to remain faithful for they shall receive their reward. They shall receive a white robe, a name in the Lamb's Book of Life and a name confessed before the Father and His Angels.

The Faithful Church

Philadelphia Revelation 3:7-13

The meaning of the word Philadelphia is brotherly love. It describes the charity and brotherly fellowship that dissipates the bitter personal animosities that characterized the theological disputants of the Sardis Period. It made the evangelistic and missionary labors of the past 150 years possible. This church was located on the main route from Rome to the east. It was a place of great opportunity to spread the gospel. Jesus describes Himself in verse 7 as holy. Referencing His character which is holy and separated from sin. Philadelphia was strategically located in the hub of a busy city on a main highway. It was a place that was free to preach the gospel to the lost. Jesus provided an open opportunity to the church at Philadelphia. Christ opened doors of the ministry that no man could shut. Three things are said of this church. It had a little strength. It was like a person coming back to life who was still very weak. It was the dead Sardis Church revived. Revivals have been characteristic of the Philadelphia Period.

These Revivals began with George Whitefield in AD 1739, followed by John Wesley, Charles G. Finney and D. L. Moody. It had set before it an open door that no man could shut. Note: This promise was made by Him, who "hath the Key of David, He that openeth' and no man shutteth ; and 'shutteth' and no man openeth." In 1793, William Carey sailed for India, where he found an "open door." Since then the Lord has opened the doors into China, Japan, Korea, India, Africa and the isles of the sea. He will continue until there is not a country in the world where the missionary cannot go. The Church at Philadelphia is still in existence. The only one of the Seven Churches that has survived. While it suffered more or less under the "Ten Persecutions" of the "Smyrna Period," it has never yet suffered in a persecution that was world-wide.

This "hour of temptation" must be impending and doubtlessly refers to the "Great Tribulation" that is to come upon the whole world. Occurring before the return of the Lord to set up His Millennial Kingdom. The promise is that the "Philadelphia Church" shall not pass through the Tribulation. The "Philadelphia Period" covers the time between AD 1750 and AD 1900. The characteristics of all these time periods continue on in the church down to the end. The Evangelistic and Missionary movements of the "Philadelphia Period" are now more mechanical and based on business methods; possessing less spiritual power. This will continue until Christ returns. Christ privileged this church because they kept God's word not denying His name. Revelation 3:9 (NKJV) states "9 Indeed I will make those of the synagogue of Satan, who say they are Jews and are not, but lie—indeed I will make them come and worship before your feet, and to know that I have loved you." (Nelson, 1982) This church loved Christ and therefore their enemies will fall before them. As Christians, we are not to be distracted from the calling and purpose in which God has given.

The Lukewarm Church

Laodicea Revelation 3:14-22

This church's conduct was repulsive to Christ. Verses 15-16 (KJV) states "I know thy works, that thou art neither cold nor hot: I would thou wert cold or hot. So then, because thou art lukewarm and neither cold nor hot, I will spue thee out of my mouth." (*Nelson, 1982*) Christ has no commendation for this church, however, He does have much to complain of. This was the last of the Seven Churches in Asia Minor. The message to this church was clear and authoritative. In verse 14, Jesus called Himself the "Amen." Amen is the final word in which He is warning them and letting this church know that this was their last and final chance. The churches of today are largely in the state of "lukewarmness." This condition shows very little warm-hearted spirituality.

These churches have Cathedral-like buildings, stained glass windows, eloquent preachers, paid singers and large congregations. Many of these activities are largely mechanical and of a social character. Some of them have amassed large landed interests, are well endowed and yet they are poor in spirit. Revival meetings are held, but instead of waiting on the Lord for power, evangelists and paid singers are hired to put on a show; winning souls have become a business. The cause of this lukewarmness is the same as self-deception as seen in the church of Laodicea. They thought they were rich and outwardly they were, but Christ saw the poverty of their heart. The Church at Laodicea was not burdened with debt, but it was most assuredly burdened with wealth. This church was near-sighted because they could only see their prosperity. However, they were short-sighted as it related to heavenly things. The Lord counseled them to anoint their eyes with eye salve. Their merchants sold ointments and herbs that possessed a high degree of healing virtue. However, they possessed no spiritual salve that would restore impaired spiritual vision. Only by the unction of the Holy Spirit could this be accomplished. In verses 18-19 (KJV) "I counsel thee to buy from Me gold tried in the fire, that thou mayest be rich, and white raiment, that thou mayest be clothed and that the shame of nakedness may not appear, and anoint thine eyes with eye salve, that thou mayest see."

The eye salve signifies medicine that heals the eyes so they would not be spiritually blind and that they might get their sight back. Jesus desired the best for them and was giving this church a cure for their sickness. He is offering His invitation to come into their hearts and come to Him in repentance. Jesus does not want us to be lukewarm but continually on fire and drawing others to Him. Revelation 3:19-22 *(KJV)* "19 As many as I love, I rebuke and chasten. Therefore, be zealous and repent. 20 Behold, I stand at the door and knock. If anyone hears My voice and opens the door, I will come into him and dine with him, and he with Me. 21 To him who overcomes I will grant to sit with Me on My throne, as I also overcame and sat down with My Father on His throne. 22 "He who has an ear, let him hear what the Spirit says to the churches."

(Nelson, 1982)

At the end of each letter, we read: "Let him hear what the Spirit says to the churches." Thus, the Lord speaks to the church as a whole. The Seven Churches do not represent seven time periods since the ascension of Jesus. These Seven Churches as well as churches today represent the experience and conditions of Christianity. Our current spiritual condition or personal experience determines which church we are in. The messages and promises given to the Seven Churches are timeless and universal. These Seven Churches have taught us what kind of church Jesus wants us to be and the things we should avoid. We must understand that we are the church.

These are the following characteristics Jesus wants His church to have: Obedience to His word, Being energetic for Christ, Endurance against opposition, Sound in doctrine, Willingness to be tireless in labor, Courageous in the face of death, Motivated by love, Trusting God, Serving the needs of others, Continuously growing spiritually, Numerically, Pure and Holy, Having no tolerance for false teaching and Reprove those who are living in sin, Be zealous and stable, Willing and able to practice self-evaluation, Always putting God first and Having Jesus as the center of their life. There is a comforting promise for those who remain faithful. We will get to sit with Christ and enjoy all the benefits of Heaven. This is a promise to every faithful Christian if we listen to what the Spirit of the Lord is saying and hold fast to His name.

Even during these uncertain times, the bible teaches us that according to Matthew 24:13 (KJV) "But he that shall endure unto the end, the same shall be saved." Galatians 6:9 (KJV): "And let us not be weary in well doing: for in due season we shall reap, if we faint not." Hebrews 10:36 (KJV) states "For you have need of endurance, so that after you have done the will of God, you may receive the promise:" The enemy is a master of using sin to discourage, disappoint and destroy us. For this very reason, we must recognize things that hinder our spiritual growth and be aware of the schemes, ploys and plots of Satan. We must not allow ourselves to be entangled in bondage which we have been set free from. Hebrews 12:1 (KJV) "Wherefore seeing we also are compassed about with so great a cloud of witnesses, let us lay aside every weight, and the sin which doth so easily beset us, and let us run with patience the race that is set before us."

Valleys

Speaking from personal experience, I thought I only had the one issue of unforgiveness. However, over the course of my life, God revealed to me that I have encountered some deep-rooted issues that spawned unforgiveness. I struggled with fear, shame, guilt, emotional pain, rejection, loss, abandonment, isolation, loneliness, depression and anxiety. Other issues included intimidation, infidelity, unworthiness, oppression, depression, mental, physical and sexual abuse, low self-esteem, mistreatment and persecution. I was a beautiful disaster or as some may say, a "hot mess." I didn't know how to solve my problems until the day I had a personal encounter with Jesus. Before then, I suppressed a lot of my feelings not realizing that I needed healing and deliverance. I was broken and sunken into my lowest valley. I wanted God to use me, but if I was to be used by Him; I knew I had to endure my valley experience. He used the same issues that broke me to make me whole again; I wanted to live. The enemy could have used my valley moments to destroy me, but God had a bigger plan for my life. Through my repentance and genuine submission to Him, He first dealt with the issues of my heart. This laid the foundation. I realized that I could no longer ride the coattail of my ministering mother or great-grandmother. It was finally time for me to get to know God for myself.

In life, people will encounter peaks and valleys experiences.

While both are essential for our growth and spiritual maturity; in this hour I will limit this book for now by discussing valleys. According to Webster's Revised Unabridged Dictionary a valley is defined as the space enclosed between ranges of hills or mountains, or the strip of land at the bottom of the depressions intersecting a country, which usually includes the bed of a stream. Containing frequently broad alluvial plains on one or both sides of the stream." There are several valleys mentioned in the bible that I will reference." "The Lord Jesus leads home many sons to glory. We have to pass through an infinite variety of circumstances, and they are not always mountain top experiences. There are valleys that are sometimes very deep. The God who is victorious in 1 Kings 20, is the same God who has begun a good work in you and will perform it until the day of Jesus Christ (Phil. 1:6) (NKJV).

The Valley of Elah

"And the Philistines stood on one side of the mountain, Israel stood on the other side and there was a valley between them. And Saul and the men of Israel were gathered together, and they encamped in the valley of Elah, and drew up in battle array against the Philistines. "(1 Sam. 17:2 (NKJV)

Most of us will have some familiarity with this valley. Here we find a full-length portrait of the enemy of our souls, represented by Goliath of Gath. Mighty in all his armor with his armor bearer going before him. When he made the challenge to Israel they were dismayed and greatly afraid. I don't think anyone who walks with God in sobriety will fail to have some thoughts concerning their frailty. Look at Paul, his armor could not protect him. Who is the enemy of our souls? By the time we come to Revelation 20:2 his identity is fully revealed, "the dragon, that old serpent, which is the Devil and Satan." He is too much for man, in our own power we cannot handle the devil alone; we need Jesus! Indeed, in Jude 1:9 (NKJV) we read, "Yet Michael the archangel, in contending with the devil, when he disputed about the body of Moses, dared not bring against him a reviling accusation, but said, The Lord rebuke you."

Take account of the way in which Saul went. His armor would not do to defend him. The Lord God selected five smooth stones for David's sling. The stones chosen by the Lord God were symbolic of the weapons He chose to deal with our enemies. How do we allow the Lord God to deal with the enemy of our souls today? We have to get down on our knees and pray. It is very attractive when we consider the Lord Jesus dealing with the enemy of our souls; how He selected exactly the right stones to deal with David. Not all five stones were 'used', as it were, in the temptation, but only three. Then in the garden another was used when He said, "Not my will but Thine be done." In a world where man does his own will (sin is lawlessness); here was a man who is utterly devoted to God's will and that stone, rightly directed, brought the giant down. 1 Samuel 17:51 (NKJV), Therefore David ran and stood over the Philistine, took his sword and drew it out of its sheath and killed him, and cut off his head with it. And when the Philistine saw that their champion was dead, they fled"

David returned to Jerusalem with the head of Goliath and put the armor of the giant in his tent (there was still more work to do). Saul asked Abner, "Whose son is he?" He could not answer. But we can now answer the question. It is the Father's only Begotten Son in whom He is well pleased, Jehovah's Servant, God's King. He has met the adversary and shortly He is going to undo his works. Luke 11:22 (NKJV) "But when a stronger than he comes upon him and overcomes him, he takes from him all his armor in which he trusted and divides his spoils." We can rejoice, dearly beloved, not only in the valley but also in the God of the valley. Who is He? It is Jesus, who has met the enemy and defeated him, spoiled principalities and powers, now at God's right hand with all power in heaven and earth given to Him.

The Valley of the Shadow of Death

"Yea, though I walk through the valley of the shadow of death, I will fear no evil; for You are with me; Your rod and Your staff, they comfort me " Psalm 23:4 (NKJV) I would like to briefly introduce you to the second valley. A valley described by another word in Hebrew; the Valley of Hinnom. If any of you have been to Israel and down to Petra, you will know exactly what I am talking about. This is the kind of valley where the bottom is only a length of fifteen to twenty feet across; maybe less. However, the walls can rise as high as eight hundred feet and are very close together. This prohibits the sun from reaching the bottom of the valley, causing it to become very dark.

This valley is not unique as there are many examples in the Judean foothills. When traveling through the old road from Jerusalem to Jericho you will see some examples of this type of valley. Have you ever pondered the time when David fled from Saul, just how close he seemed to get; but was never able to catch him. David knew these valleys were excellent hiding places. Be that as it may, this was a very dangerous place for sheep because wolves, lions and bears also dwelt in this valley. Let us use this valley to discuss the safety in Psalm 23. In the first three verses of Psalm 23, David speaks about the Shepherd - "the Lord is my shepherd, I shall not want", but when he gets down to verse 4 he no longer talks about the Shepherd, he talks to the Shepherd. "Thy rod and thy staff they comfort me"? The rod is composed of a piece of wood which is approximately two feet long with a bulb and perhaps a nail. The rod is a tremendous weapon against wild beasts. If you are in the hands of a shepherd who loves you so much that he is prepared to give his life for you; you are safe. Jesus is that shepherd. We can approach the valley of the shadow of death in all confidence.

Some connect the valley of the shadow of death only with the circumstances of death, but rather it seems to me that it represents the whole of our pathway, all is connected with danger, but safety is found in Him who is the Shepherd, the God of the valley.

The Valley of Baca

"Blessed is the man whose strength is in You, whose heart is set on pilgrimage. As they pass through the Valley of Baca, they make it a spring; The rain also covers it with pools." Psalm 84:5-6 (NKJV) This valley has personally occasioned me a great deal. If you look up the best Biblical map you can find, you will discover that against the valley of Baca there is an entry known as - "situation unknown." If you move amongst the Saints of God and get closer to the burdens that they carry, you will discover, there are many places of weeping. Like the Valley of Baca, these situations are also unknown. There are even many areas of sadness amongst the Saints of God that are unidentified. Trials and burdens that nobody else knows about. There are a lot of tears in this world - that is what Baca literally means, "lamentation" and "weeping." National disasters cause weeping amongst worldly men and women, but there is also a good deal of weeping amongst saints.

Jeremiah also known as "the weeping prophet of the nations" closed his dispensation. Let us look briefly into the matter of tears in the Bible. We read about tears of remorse - Esau sought the blessing with tears (Hebrews 12:17), but remorse did not yield any results for him. Malachi also covered the altar with unavailing tears and remorse (Malachi 2:13). However, there are more heartfelt tears such as those of the woman in (Luke 7). Like the tears of repentance shed at the blessed feet of the Lord Jesus with which she washed His feet. But let us also consider the tears of a servant, "He who continually goes forth weeping, bearing seed for sowing, Shall doubtless come again with rejoicing, Bringing his sheaves with him. Psalm 126:6 (NKJV) Paul in serving the Lord in all humbleness of spirit in Ephesus wept for three years night and day (Acts 20:31). Timothy was a man of genuine compassion. A great example of how the saints should love and forgive one another. Where did he learn this? Probably from Paul. Paul yearned over the Ephesians. He also wrote to the Corinthians "out of much affliction and anguish of heart with many tears" (2 Corinthians. 2:4).

In (John 11) Jesus shed tears of silent expression with deep feelings. The Lord cried out in tears (Hebrews 5:7). This is the God of the valleys. Thank God we have One who draws near to us. Even when our brethren or our nearest and dearest cannot understand. There is always One who delights to draw near. It is in these circumstances dearly beloved, we learn how precious is the Man of Sorrows. It is against this background that we can begin to appreciate (Psalm 84). "Blessed is the man whose strength is in Thee". This is not the natural man, it is the man of faith. The man of God who is drawing his resources from another sphere knows his God. The man had Old Testament limitations in his knowledge of course, nevertheless, he could say "For the LORD God is a sun and shield; The LORD will give grace and glory; No good thing will he withhold from those who walk uprightly" (Psalm 84:11). He knows where he is going - "How amiable are thy tabernacles" (v.1), "Blessed are they that dwell in thy house" (v.4) - he wants, he longs, to be there, but in the meantime we read "Blessed is the man whose strength is in thee; in whose heart are the ways of them" (v.5). He realizes he has a path through these various circumstances for the education of his soul. He understands it and he accepts it. Are we going to kick against the sorrows, are we going to hit out or are we going to be exercised? This man is exercised and passing through the valley of Baca. He finds a well and is refreshed by the God of the valleys. But that is not the end, "the rain also filleth the pools," there is education and liberation for the whole church of God. In (2 Corinthians 4:1) the Apostle Paul stated that he endured all of this. Why? That he might be able to comfort the saints as he was comforted by God. It is tremendously encouraging to belong to the family of God. As the God of the Valley, He is available in any circumstance and available to the body of Christ.

The Valley of Achor

"And Joshua, and all Israel with him, took Achan the son of Zerah, and the silver, and the garment, and the wedge of gold, and his sons, and his daughters, and his oxen, and his asses, and his sheep, and his tent, and all that he had: and they brought them unto the valley of Achor. And Joshua said, why hast thou troubled us? the LORD shall trouble thee this day. And all Israel stoned him with stones, and burned them with fire, after they had stoned them with stones. And they raised over him a great heap of stones unto this day. So, the LORD turned from the fierceness of his anger. Wherefore the name of that place was called, The valley of Achor, unto this day." (Joshua 7:24-26) (KJV) There is no difficulty in identifying this valley on the map or in scriptures. The only difficulty about this valley is that we cannot always identify it in our individual or collective experiences. Geographically it is located near the Red Sea. When reading about it in (Joshua 7) and (Hosea 2) it is referred to as "the door of hope." Achor is the place where sin is confessed, judged and put away. It is very important to understand more about it.

Historically, when the children of Israel came over Jordan, they had a tremendous victory at Jericho. The next place was Ai and they sent only three thousand men thinking it was a small place. The people of God were defeated before the people of Ai and thirty-six died. In Joshua 7 (KJV) we find Joshua with the elders of the children of Israel on their faces before the Lord crying, 'What shall we do? would to God we had been content and dwelt on the other side of Jordan!' Before we are too hard on Israel let us recognize that this is the language of many hearts today. Ah, but the Lord said to Joshua, "Get thee up; wherefore liest thou thus upon thy face? Israel hath sinned." They were to confess their sin and deal with it. Joshua coveted a goodly Babylonish garment, silver and gold and had hidden them in his tent, causing the victory of God to be halted. In the mercy of God that sin was brought out into the open, confessed, dealt with drastically, judged and put away. Ai became the second city of victory in the triumphant march of Israel through the promised land. In (Hosea 2) we get the prophetic picture in regard to Israel in the coming day. They are also guilty of sin, in that they have crucified their Messiah. In this chapter, sometimes called 'the Luke 16 of the Old Testament', God brings His people into the wilderness and there He speaks to their hearts. The steps of recovery in Israel are three - lamentation, confession and response. The door of hope is in their confession and putting away of the sin, which we read about in (Zechariah 12:12-14) (NKJV), "And the land shall mourn, every family by itself: the family of the house of David by itself, and their wives by themselves; the family of the house of Nathan by itself, and their wives by themselves; the family of the house of Levi by itself, and their wives by themselves; all the families that remain, every family by itself, and their wives by themselves."

There they are in their mourning and confession. Zechariah 13:1, "In that day a fountain shall be opened for the house of David and for the inhabitants of Jerusalem, for sin and for uncleanness." The valley of Achor for a door of hope. This is right up to date. If there is hope with us, we have the ability to bring sin out into the open and confess it. I believe we will still prove that He despises not the exercises of His people, "a broken and a contrite heart - These, O God, You will not despise" Psalm 51:17 (NKJV).

Dr. Tomeka Wooten

The Valley of Berachah

"And on the fourth day they assembled themselves in the valley of Berachah; for there they blessed the LORD: therefore the name of the same place was called, The valley of Berachah, unto this day." (2 Chronicles 20:26) This is a very happy and precious valley, mentioned as another chapter of victory. This is a prophetic chapter. There are features in it that carry teachings that are referable to things which must shortly come to pass. The world to come will be introduced by judgments. Babylon, religious and commercial (Revelation 17 and 18) first, then the Western powers next, the Arab powers third and Russia fourth.

This chapter deals with some of the prophetic elements that are found in connection with the Arab states in the coming day. You remember how the king of the north will come down in an overflowing scourge (Daniel 11) and he is found in Egypt. There he hears tidings out of the east and out of the north (probably the eastern powers and the western powers being dealt with by God at Armageddon - Revelation 16) and he returns towards Jerusalem. Then as he gets as far as the valley of Berachah news reaches Israel (Jehoshaphat) that there is this great army waiting to overrun Jerusalem. This reminds us of Psalm 46. The Lord will have partially intervened for His people, so they are encouraged to "Be still and know that I am God." Although the army was only twenty-five miles from Jerusalem, Jehoshaphat approached this situation in a dignified way and called for a fast. Then there was a great prayer meeting in Judea. Jehoshaphat and the whole city gathered in the temple court. Can you picture them? There were no absentees from that prayer meeting. The wives and the little ones all stood before the Lord with real, earnest prayer. Jehoshaphat prayed like a man who was accustomed to praying. He quoted the Scripture, bringing the situation into focus. It must have been a very moving occasion. This was a prayer meeting that turned into a word of ministry, for the prophet Jahazial spoke; "Hearken ye, all Judah, and ye inhabitants of Jerusalem, and thou king Jehoshaphat, Thus saith the LORD unto you, Be not afraid nor dismayed by reason of this great multitude; for the battle is not yours, but God's." They fell down in worship, and they lifted up their voice and praised the Lord. What a happy prayer meeting. On the next day they went out to meet the great host and Jehoshaphat "consulted with the people." Some leaders are in danger of steamrolling the saints, but here was one who called in the saints. He consulted with the people and they appointed singers to go before the army. The praise was too much for the enemy. "God dwells in the praises of His people" (Psalm 22:3).

The enemy oftentimes attacks our praise and if that is missing the enemy gets an advantage. It was not so with Jehoshaphat. They appointed singers in the front line that went out against the enemy. We get the delightful picture like so many times repeated in Scripture. When the enemy began to slay one another, the children of Ammon and the children of Moab, stood up against the children of Seir and slew them. When they had dealt with them, they slew one another. I am not quite sure how many references there are (I think about six). This is God's approved method of dealing with the opposition; praise is given to the Lord and the enemy begins to slay one another. In the valley of Berachah when the Moabites and Ammonites, together with some of the Meunites, came up against Jehoshaphat and Judah.

They looked upon them, they were all dead corpses, just as in (Exodus 15). They stripped them of their precious things and it took them three days to gather in the spoils because it was so much. Israel had a session of praise on the battlefield before returning to Jerusalem. They went to the very place they started from, the temple. This incident started with prayer and ended with praise. We can see this picture of the valley of Berachah and the intervention of the God of the valley Jehoshaphat. No doubt a picture of One greater than he. Jehosophat and all the men of Judah and Jerusalem were in the temple leading the praise; the song going up to the God who has blessed His people in valley conditions.

The God of the Valleys

In 1 Kings 20 we saw that God in His grace came in for a people who said "The Lord He is God; the Lord He is God. Graciously victory is given to Israel, the God of the hills and the God of the valleys. However, there is one character in this chapter who I view as utterly despicable; that man is Ahab. He did more to provoke Jehovah to anger than any other king in Israel. He sold himself to do evil and his wife Jezebel stirred him up. You may not have noticed in the first victory (when God was declared to be the God of the hills) with thirty-three kings against him, Ahab came not in the forefront of the battle but in the rear. Who shall order the battle? It is set in motion by the young men, the servants of the prince of the provinces. These two hundred and thirty-two men went out to battle. When the seven thousand men went to battle, they were victorious. Only when Ahab sees that the enemy has been routed he joins them to celebrate the victory; despicable I say. When we come to the God of the Valleys, God has given a signal of victory. Israel slew a hundred thousand footmen in one day. Twenty seven thousand more attempted to flee but were killed when a wall fell on them; tremendous intervention. Then we find an encounter between Ben-hadad and Ahab. Ben-hadad, is a religious type of the kings of Syria, he was an idol worshiper. Ahab said to this idol worshiper, "he is my brother" (v.32), for he too was an idol worshiper.

Here we find the test at the close of our talk together. Where is your heart? Where is mine? Are we just going to stand by and see these victories? God proved to be the God of the hills and the God of the valleys. Are we going to be spectators; are we? It depends altogether, dearly beloved brethren, as to whether your heart and mine are taken up with the idols of this world. Are we lovers of pleasure, lovers of money and lovers of ourselves? In devotion our hearts should go out to Him; who is the God of the valleys, the God of the hills, our precious Savior and Lord. The God of the hills and valleys, our God has been fully revealed in the Lord Jesus. The final test is what is in your heart and what is in my heart. "My son, give me thine heart, and let thine eyes observe my ways" (Proverbs 23:26). Let our affections flow out to Him who is worthy to be praised." (*Patterson, n.d.*)

"Valleys are symbolic and are often associated with battles, unfaithfulness, negativity, and punishment. However, valleys are also symbolic of beauty, strength, victory, treasures, hope, blessings and fertility. Deuteronomy 8:7 (NKJV) is followed by a description of the fertility of the land of promise. "For the Lord your God is bringing you into a good land, a land of brooks of water, of fountains and springs, that flow out of valleys and hills." Deuteronomy 8:7 (NKJV).

"A land of wheat and barley, of vines and fig trees and pomegranates, a land of olive oil and honey, a land in which you will eat bread without scarcity, in which you will lack nothing; a land whose stones are iron and out of whose hills you can dig copper." Deuteronomy 8:8-9 (NKJV).

The capacity to grow crops there is understandable, for the Hebrew term found in the Deuteronomic context (biqàa,,) is most commonly used to "refer to broad plains/valleys that were not located in the mountains."

When the Philistines were returning the ark to Israelite territory, the residents of Beth Shemesh "were harvesting wheat in the valley" (1 Samuel 6:13). The specific Hebrew term used here (àemeq) is most commonly translated as "valley" or "plain." Most likely referred to an area, although wide, is not as broad as the term deep used in Deuteronomy 8:7 and 11:11. This same term is used by the psalmist in praising God whose loving care saw to it that "the valleys are covered with grain" (Psalm. 65:13).

Those sent by Moses to spy out the land of promise found grapes growing there (Numbers 13:23-24). In a later time of drought, King Ahab sent his servant to look for water and grazing land for his animals. "Ahab told Obadiah, 'Go through the land in all the springs and valleys. Maybe we can find some grazing areas so we can keep the horses and mules alive and not have to kill them" (1 Kings 18:5). In both cases the Hebrew term employed most commonly refers to an area formed by a temporary river that flows at times with great force in the rainy season. But provides a dry channel in the summer. The fact that the water table was higher in such an area allowed for plant growth. For example, the lover declares to the beloved, "I went down to the orchard of walnut trees, to look for the blossoms of the valley to see if the vines had budded or if the pomegranates were in bloom" (Song of Solomon 6:11). 8 The Hebrew word (nah£al) in all three cases refers to narrower valleys (often rendered "wadis) that could be cultivated." (*Patterson R. D., n.d.*)

What the Enemy Meant for Bad

In 2010, at my uncle's funeral held in Washington D.C., I rededicated my life to Christ and was baptized again. What the enemy meant for bad, God will turn around for the good of those that love him and called according to His purpose. God overcame the world. He uses our afflictions and adversities that by trusting in Him, having faith and through His strength, we may overcome as well. God will use us in His kingdom. Allowing us to be the voice for others that He may get all the glory! It came down to a choice and I wanted to be counted worthy and saved.

We can expect to experience everything on this earth that God's own Son did. We must understand that when we go through trials and tribulations, they bring forth patience, patience brings forth experience and experience brings forth HOPE! Even in this dark and perilous world, there is peace in having hope that one day when He returns; we know we are going home to be with the Father. I have seen and experienced the Glory of God and I know that He has brought me a mighty long way. I have been in accidents, doctors have given me bad reports and so called incurable medical diagnosis, uncertain prognosis, but God covered me and healed me of my afflictions. People have hurt me and never offered an apology. The Holy Spirit intercedes for me; when I was hurt and did not know what to pray for. He was and still is my comforter and protector. He has given me a peace beyond my own understanding, and He kept me from what could have been. Through my afflictions and adversity, I learned how to have a right relationship with Him. I learned what to fight for and what to let go. Most of all, I learned how to pray. He has given me knowledge, revelation, wisdom and understanding. Showing me the way and the truth. I learned how to navigate through the valleys and its rough terrain. Even in the valleys, when matters look extremely bleak, God's people experience His provision.

No Weapon Formed

I was told that my mother was kicked in her belly when she was nine months pregnant with me. Also, when I was six years old, I can remember begging to stay at my grandmother's house with my younger cousins. I wanted to sleep over, but I had school and my mother wouldn't let me. That very weekend I lost my cousins in a house fire at my grandmother's home. I lost three cousins, all babies and a great aunt due to a house fire. Had I been there, I would probably have died too. The only survivors were my grandmother and a male cousin one year younger than myself, but no weapon formed against me prospered.

When Satan came to me as a child with seeds of suggestions, they immediately took root. He made me think the worst of myself. I was ugly, unwanted and unloved is what the enemy told me at an incredibly early age. He wanted me dead. His plan was to kill, steal and destroy me but God! Yes, God had another plan! He may have made me think of all the worst, but God illuminated my best. I was innocent and did not understand what was going on, but somebody was praying for me and to God be all the Glory! If we are not careful, sin creeps into our heart to take over. Sin separates us from God and is a false comforter. I despised change and was easily offended and aggravated. God started pulling back the layers of my life because He wanted to expose those roots so He can deal with them, so that I may be healed and delivered. The Holy Spirit was teaching me how to seek His face, cast down, loose, bind and destroy generational curses. Breaking the yokes of bondage, that I may be free and whole. Becoming a testimony to others and being used for His Glory. In the past, I used to stick to what I knew. I chose familiar bondage over a foreign freedom because it felt so good in the moment; until it did not. It was false, it was not lasting nor was it real. Satan is a liar and deceiver, cunning, clever and crafty. Nevertheless, God is strategic. It is only God who is the true comfort. It's because of His goodness, grace and mercy, that my eyes have been awakened to my false senses of comfort. I recognized that for me, sin never brought forth truth, healing or intimacy with God, therefore these things had to be purged from me.

Even though this has been ongoing for most of my life. Once I submitted to God, allowing myself to be forgiven and forgiving others, the healing and deliverance started to take effect. Satan's attacks will still come; therefore we have to remember to always be sober minded, vigilant and ready for war. The bible states in 1 Peter 5:8 (KJV) 8" Be sober, be vigilant; because your adversary the devil, as a roaring lion, walketh about, seeking whom he may devour." One of Satan's tactics is to use fiery darts as a weapon of destruction; a spiritual assassin. A dart is an instrument of war, a light spear. "Fiery darts" (Ephesians 6:16) (NKJV) are so-called allusions which discharge darts from the bow while they are on fire or armed with some combustible material. Arrows are compared to lightning (Deuteronomy 32:23; 32:42) (NKJV) (Psalm 7:13; 120:4) (NKJV). Ephesians 6:12 (NKJV) reminds us that our fight is not with the people arrayed against us, but with the principalities, powers, rulers of the darkness of this age and spiritual hosts of wickedness. The fiery darts of the wicked one will fly and set their marks on anyone who is not clothed in their spiritual armor. These principalities often try to convince God's people that they are not good enough and not worthy. They hold up sins as evidence; trying to blackmail Christians into giving up. Fiery darts are Satan's artillery; weapons used to ultimately destroy us. How do we fight against the fiery darts that Satan uses against us? According to Ephesians 6:16 (NKJV), "Above all, taking the shield of faith, with which you will be able to quench all the fiery darts of the wicked one." Everything links back to faith. Faith is a complete confidence or trust in something or someone. The word is the main armor of defense against every attack of Satan. The Bible says according to Hebrews 11:1 (NKJV) "Now faith is the substance of things hoped for, the evidence of things not seen." We must hear, speak and live by the word that we may grow in faith. "For the weapons of our warfare are not carnal but mighty in God for pulling down strongholds." 2 Corinthians 10:4 (NKJV).

Dr. Tomeka Wooten

 Seeds

In October 2018, I had a dream that I was at my great-grandmother's house and as I came down the stairs of her front porch, I realized there was a garden. Seeds that I had planted. I was so happy to see this garden. The first thing that captured my attention was the soil. It was dark, rich, soft and fertile. Then I realized there were all sorts of vegetables growing all around such as peppers, squash, tomatoes, corn and bell peppers. At first glance I only saw the good and ripe vegetables. Then I saw that there were some rotten vegetables throughout the garden. I realized that some of the rotten ones were touching the good ones causing them to rot on the very side in which they made contact. When I had awakened from the dream, I immediately went into prayer asking God to help me understand the dream. He brought back to my remembrance Matthew 13:3-25 (NKJV) regarding seeds. Then I remembered a sermon in which Bishop Michael Burney Sr. had preached. The sermon was on the mystery of a seed. He said that seeds are the beginning of a process. A seed has the potential power and ability to multiply. To also feed, give love, bring happiness and joy.

All those things are in the hands of the individual yet powerless outside of soil. That preached word stuck with me. In the soil over the process of time, a seed goes through stages; germination. They take root in the ground, bringing forth shoots that grow into stems, eventually leaves and whatever fruit it bears.

A seed needs soil, water and sunshine to grow. Then he talked about the mystery of the seed. The mystery of the Kingdom is comparable to that of the seed. The word of the Lord is a seed. Natural fruits and vegetables are seeds, our children are our seeds, the deeds that we do, our words, thoughts, finances and our prayers, are all seeds. As for my dream, God revealed that those vegetables were comparable to people. People of the earth "the fields of ripe and ready but the labors are few." This reference Matthew 9:37-38 (KJV), "Then saith he unto his disciples, the harvest truly is plenteous, but the labourers are few; pray ye therefore the Lord of the harvest, that he will send forth labourers into the harvest."

The soil represented the foundation. There is power in the foundation. That is why in my dream, I was at my great-grandmother's house. While the other kids would be outside playing, I remember sitting at her feet while she read the bible to me. That is where my foundation began. The soil was fresh, and the ground was fertile. According to 1 Corinthians 3:7 (NKJV) "So then neither he who plants is anything, nor he who waters, but God who gives the increase." The seed was planted. God's Word went forth. It was sown and took root in my heart a long time ago. God knows who we are and who we were called to be before we were formed in our mother's womb. Some people grow up with the right conditions and environment for a seed to flourish and then there are some that don't. There are some people who are hearers only, they may know the word yet reject it; but God wants us to be hearers and doers of His Word.

There are others that do not have any foundation. They do not know God at all. That is why it is important as ambassadors for Christ that we love one another and live by example. The seeds that fall on stony ground, is ground that's not prepared. It sprouts up but has no root. When trials and tribulations come, it has nothing to hold on to; it withers. Having no root takes little to turn people away from Christ, which is where many are today. A seed sown amongst thorns may grow but is eventually choked. These people may know the word but are distracted. Thorns cannot stop the Word from going forth in a person's life, but it can slow the productivity of their growth in Christ. Partying instead of praying, having other lovers, rebellion, worrying about the cares of the world, idols, doubt and fear are distractions that will delay productivity in Christ. Then there is good ground where the productivity comes in different degrees (30, 60, 100-fold). It all depends on how much you cooperate with God, your relationship, faith and devotion to Him. It is all about the principle that you practice, the seed, the soil, what it produces and the measure of production. Be mindful and watch your thoughts, every action starts as a thought. Watch what you allow to enter your eye and ear gates. Guard your heart from any contamination. Rot can contaminate your spirit. Watch the company you keep because there are some people that are great imitators. They seek to deceive, but you can't deceive the Holy Spirit! They do not know God; they just want what they want. Pray to have eyes that are not deceived. Mathew 13:24-30 (NKJV) states the wheat and tear shall grow together until harvest time and God will do the separating. The world is full of good and bad. As children of God, we must ask ourselves, what are we fertilizing our seeds with? What are we feeding our spirit? Is it soil, water, sunshine or manure? Is our heart rotten? Are we contaminated and are we contaminating others? Are we the wheat or a tare? Are we ready and ripe waiting on our harvest?

"Seeds come in different shapes and sizes, with each type having different requirements for germination (the process in which seeds sprout and begin to grow). Under the right conditions, this perfect little "package" will grow and develop into a wonderful new plant. This plant can provide food, shelter or beauty. There are five basic physical conditions that all seeds need to germinate; light, water, soil, time and temperature. Christians need these same five spiritual conditions to grow. Look at how and why a seed needs each of these conditions and how they spiritually apply to a Christian's life. Sunlight, which changes in length and intensity throughout the year, is a plant's signal to start germinating at the right time. It also helps show the plant which way is up and where to send its leaves to receive light, so that it can produce its own food. Notice what Psalm 119:105 (NKJV) states: "Your word is a lamp unto my feet, And a light to my path." In His Word, God shows us through daily bible study which way to go.

Alone, man does not know how to direct his own steps (Jeremiah 10:23) (NKJV). As a result, he gropes in the darkness of this world, ignorant of the only way that produces true and lasting peace, happiness and prosperity. The light of God's Word reveals the path that leads to the Kingdom of God and eternal life. Water is also a vital key for the life of a plant. Some seeds need to be immersed in water to germinate. All seeds need to absorb and fill up with water, which is the first step in germination. This happens by either a chemical trigger or a change in the seed coat.

This is an obvious parallel to baptism. When one is immersed in water and upon receiving God's Spirit, a new life begins. Additionally, water is likened to the Holy Spirit which we need to ask for and be replenished with daily if we are to survive. John 4:14 (NKV). A Christian's goal is to become full of God's Spirit. Soil will determine the health and strength of a plant. The better the soil, the healthier and stronger the plant. The soil should not be too sandy or too hard and it must supply the right nutrients for the plant to grow strong. In addition, temperature is important in the germination process. If a seed is in an environment lacking the right temperature, its chance of success is severely limited; even if all the other elements are present.

Many Christians today have a "temperature" problem. In Revelation 3:15-16 (NKJV) Christ warns His people, "I know your works, that you are neither cold nor hot. I could wish you were cold or hot. So then, because you are lukewarm, and neither cold nor hot, I will vomit you out of My mouth." None of us can afford to let our zeal for brotherly love and doctrinal truth wane. Therefore, we must be diligent to have and maintain the right temperature to survive this lukewarm age!

The seed's sole purpose is to reproduce its own kind. In the "parable of the sower," seed was cast upon different environments, yielding varying rates of failure and success. Christ explained that "Now the parable is this: The seed is the word of God" Luke 8:11 (NKJV). The purpose of God's Work is to cast those seeds. Each seed has the potential to grow into a new, fully mature plant. In the same way, God is reproducing His "own kind" through man. As His "firstfruits," God gave us the "seed" of His Spirit, with the potential to become like Him, having perfect character (Matthew. 5:48)." *(Denee, n.d.)*

"Growth begins with the sowing of seed. That is true in the vegetable kingdom of the earth. It is also true in the spiritual kingdom of Heaven. It is amazing how you can change your life simply by paying attention to the spiritual seed you sow daily. The Lord knows this, so He says..."Do not be deceived, God is not mocked; for whatever a man sows, that he will also reap. For he who sows to his flesh will of the flesh reap corruption, but he who sows to the Spirit will of the Spirit reap everlasting life" (Galatians 6:7-8) (NKJV).

The spiritual seed we are referring to is also faithful. If sown diligently, it will produce much fruit in due season. A seed, to be faithful, must die when it is sown. "Most assuredly, I say to you, unless a grain of wheat falls into the ground and dies, it remains alone; but if it dies, it produces much grain" John 12:24 (NKJV). We need to have the same patience and faith in sowing to the spirit as the farmer has in sowing to the earth. "Therefore, be patient, brethren, until the coming of the Lord. See how the farmer waits for the precious fruit of the earth, waiting patiently for it until it receives the early and latter rain. You also be patient. Establish your hearts, for the coming of the Lord is at hand." James 5:7-8 (NKJV).

In the same way, "And let us not grow weary while doing good, for in due season we shall reap if we do not lose heart." Galatians 6:9 (NKJV). "If you sow sparingly, you will also reap sparingly; if you sow bountifully, you will also reap bountifully." 2 Corinthians 9:6 (NKJV). Fruitfulness is one of the many characteristics of true obedience to God. Remaining in God's grace is conditional upon us being obedient and fruitful. Jesus once said, "Unless a grain of wheat falls into the earth and dies, it remains by itself alone, but if it dies, then it bears much fruit." John 12:24 (KJV). The seed undergoes a regeneration.

This experience is God's will for every human being as part of the journey of life. Paul teaches that physical death is but a prelude to a human being's metamorphosis into a far more glorious creature. Like Jesus, Paul uses the powerful analogy of the seed that dies and then rises up as a new body, namely the plant. (1 Corinthians 15:35-38) (NKJV). Paul is speaking of the resurrection. In the same way, there has to be a spiritual death and regeneration which is sometimes called conversion (Acts 3:19) (NKJV). This is a death to sin and a rebirth as a new creature in Christ (2 Corinthians 5:17) (NKJV) (Romans 6:3-13) (NKJV). This is called The Fruits of Repentance and Rebirth. A change of heart (repentance) results in a change of life (holiness). The old person is dead and buried and the new person has risen. This change should be evident as a reformed manner of life. If we sow the seeds which God supplies, we are promised that "God will increase the harvest of your righteousness" (2 Corinthians 9:10) (NKJV) so that we become "filled with the fruit of righteousness" (Philippians 1:11) (NKJV). Two of the fruit of righteousness are reconciliation and peace not only between us and God, but also between ourselves.

Among the fruits of righteousness is the conversion of others to Christ (the fruit of evangelism). Jesus spoke of this as a "harvest" (Matthew 9:36-38) (NKJV), and he who reaps that harvest "gathers fruit for eternal life" (John 4:35-36) (NKJV). Paul thought of himself as a gardener in the kingdom of God and of his labor as bearing fruit when he brought others to Christ and helped them to mature (Romans 1:13) (NKJV) (Philippians 1:21-22) (NKJV) (Philippians 4:17) (NKJV) (Colossians 1:5-6) (NKJV). "The fruit of the Spirit are love, joy, peace, longsuffering, kindness, goodness, faithfulness, gentleness and self-control." Fruits of that sort conflict with the works of the flesh. "I say then: Walk in the Spirit, and you shall not fulfill the lust of the flesh." (Galatians 5:16) (NKJV). We are to "increase and abound" in these fruits of the light (1 Thessalonians 3:12; 4:7, 10) (NKJV). As Christians when we think of bearing fruit, we cannot help but remember the phrase, the fruit of the Spirit spoken of in Galatians 5:22-23 (NKJV). "For you were once darkness, but now you are light in the Lord. Walk as children of light. ("for the fruit of the spirit is in all goodness, righteousness, and truth)." Ephesians 5:9 (NKJV).

The Fruit of the Spirit

The Fruit of the Spirit are virtues or Christian characteristics set forth by Apostle Paul in his letters to the Galatians. "The Holy Spirit first came at Pentecost (Acts 2:1-4) (NKJV). The initial arrival was accompanied by some spectacular manifestations. He transformed timid fishermen into fearless apostles of faith. Thousands were converted and the miraculous were taking place. The Holy Spirit was sent to convict us of our sins and comfort us, but also to empower us with gifts and transform us with fruit." The bible teaches us that when we receive Jesus Christ into our lives as our Lord and Savior, we become new creatures and that the spirit of God comes in and gives us new life. The bible teaches us that the Spirit of God produces the Fruit of the Spirit. The fruit of the Spirit are character changing outcomes. It is the product of the Holy Spirit that lives inside of us. The Fruit of the Spirit is produced by the Spirit and not by oneself. As we grow in Christ, the characteristics of Christ manifest in our lives thus fruit of the Spirit. Like physical fruit need time to grow and ripen, the fruit of the spirit also needs time to grow in our lives. A successful gardener must battle against weeds to harvest what has been planted, so that he may enjoy the manifestation of the fruit sown. We have to constantly battle against weeds of our lives such as sin that could choke out the work of the Spirit. The Holy Spirit gives us power to reject sin and provides a way out by the leading of the Holy Spirit. It is the Holy Spirit that constantly works to rid our lives of the acts of sinful nature. As stated before and according to Galatians 5: 19-26 (KJV) it states, "19 Now the works of the flesh are manifest, which are these; Adultery, fornication, uncleanness, lasciviousness, 20 Idolatry, witchcraft, hatred, variance, emulations, wrath, strife, seditions, heresies, 21 Envyings, murders, drunkenness, revellings, and such like: of the which I tell you before, as I have also told you in time past, that they which do such things shall not inherit the kingdom of God. 22 But the fruit of the Spirit is love, joy, peace, longsuffering, gentleness, goodness, faith, 23 Meekness, temperance: against such there is no law. 24 And they that are Christ's have crucified the flesh with the affections and lusts. 25 If we live in the Spirit, let us also walk in the Spirit. 26 Let us not be desirous of vain glory, provoking one another, envying one another." Galatians 5: 19-26 (KJV) (Nelson, 2003)

The Fruit of The Holy Spirit is a 9-fold fruit that characterizes all those who walk in it collectively. It is a representation of the Spirit of Christ as it manifests through the believer. In Galatians 5:22, all 9 attributes sum up love, joy, peace, long suffering, gentleness, goodness, faith, meekness and temperance. I will discuss each characteristic in an attempt to reveal the Fruit of the Spirit and what each characteristic is in detail. "The first three fruit focus on your relationship with God. The second three fruit focus on your relationship with others. The final three fruit focus on the individual." (Fruit of the Holy Spirit, 1998) "The Fruit of the Spirit therefore flow out of obedience which is walking in the spirit and walking in the light. Walking in obedience means resisting the flesh and the works of the flesh, openness to the spirit, willing to accept His rebukes and new ways of obedience and following Christ." (Kendall, 1996, 1998, 1999, 2000, 2002, 2014) Prayer is what cultivates the fruit of the spirit. As you seek the word of God, He allows the love of God to increase in your life. We know that the bible teaches that God so loved the world that He gave His only Begotten Son. We also know that God commands us to love one another.

You have to have love to exemplify the fruit of the Spirit. "[34] But when the Pharisees had heard that he had put the Sadducees to silence, they were gathered together. [35] Then one of them, which was a lawyer, asked him a question, tempting him, and saying, [36] Master, which is the great commandment in the law [37] Jesus said unto him, Thou shalt love the Lord thy God with all thy heart, and with all thy soul, and with all thy mind. [38] This is the first and great commandment. [39] And the second is like unto it, Thou shalt love thy neighbour as thyself. [40] On these two commandments hang all the law and the prophets." Matthew 22:34-40 (Nelson, 2003) "And we have known and believed the love that God hath to us. God is love; and he that dwelleth in love dwelleth in God, and God in him." 1 John 4:16 (Nelson, 2003)

Dr. Tomeka Wooten

 Love

In 1 Corinthians 13:4-13 (NKJV) states "4 Love suffers long and is kind; love does not envy; love does not parade itself, is not puffed up; 5 does not behave rudely, does not seek its own, is not provoked, thinks no evil; 6 does not rejoice in iniquity, but rejoices in the truth; 7 bears all things, believes all things, hopes all things, endures all things; 8 Love never fails. But whether there are prophecies, they will fail; whether there are tongues, they will cease; whether there is knowledge, it will vanish away. 9 For we know in part, and we prophesy in part. 10 But when that which is perfect has come, then that which is in part will be done away.11 When I was a child, I spoke as a child, I understood as a child, I thought as a child; but when I became a man, I put away childish things. 12 For now we see in a mirror, dimly, but then face to face. Now I know in part, but then I shall know just as I also am known. 13 And now abide faith, hope, love, these three; but the greatest of these is love." 1 Corinthians 13:4-13 (NKJV) (*Nelson, 2003*)

"In the Greek, there are three words which describe love. Eros means sensual love. Philia is love between friends and Agape love describes a supernatural love such as God's love for us." (*Graham, 2011*) God's unconditional and intense love for fallen humanity motivated the plan of salvation. Salvation is God making us whole or complete. "Greater love hath no man than this, that a man lay down his life for his friends." John 15:13 (KJV) God loved the world that He gave His only begotten son. What greater love? We have been commanded to love one another. The very nature of God is love. His life and holiness are based upon and are an expression of his love. "8 He who does not love does not know God, for God is love." 1 John 4:8 (NKJV) Love is the greatest gift of all. God's children are the conduits of His love.

Joy

There is a difference between joy and happiness. Happiness is an emotion. God never intended for people to be in any consistent state of emotion. Feelings that depend on something good happening is an emotion. God does want us to be happy, but His greater desire is that we have unconditional joy. Summarized in John 15:11 (NKJV), Jesus said His joy would "remain in you" and "your joy might be full and no man taketh our joy. There is "a time to weep and a time to laugh; a time to mourn, and a time to dance" Ecclesiastes 3:4 (KJV) (*Nelson, 2003*). Biblical joy is the true joy that comes from filling the spiritual void with good relationships. God wants us to have an intimate relationship with Him which brings pure joy. Jesus put it this way: "I am the vine, you are the branches. He who abides in Me, and I in him, bears much fruit; for without me you can do nothing." John 15:5 (NKJV) That fruit includes much joy! Joy is the mind's pleasure, a state of mind that is eventually felt within the heart. Therefore, we shall not pursue happiness. We are to pursue the things that are pleasing to God, and this will give us joy. Summarized in 1 Timothy 6:11 (NKJV), Paul instructs us to, "follow after righteousness, godliness, faith, love, patience, meekness." We are incapable of seeking joy apart from these things. It is pointless; it is like harvesting fruit from a tree without roots. It can't be done. However, wherever these things are found and are growing, God's pleasure will rest over the heart, and that is precisely the believer's joy. Joy is a result of obedience. Love is not puffed up, not even over joy. The joy of a person who lives in the fear of God will become increasingly and firmly anchored in God. To have joy, you have to walk in the truth; then joy will be the fruit of a life in godly fear. To have joy is to have freedom through the Holy Spirit. Where the Spirit of the Lord, there is liberty which is freedom and joy in the Lord. The Bible states "I have no greater joy than to hear that my children walk in truth." 3 John 1:4 (NKJV) (Nelson, 2003) Joy and happiness come much more from giving and serving than from getting.

The Apostle Paul reminded us that Jesus Christ had taught this very thing according to Scripture: "It is more blessed to give than to receive" Acts 20:35 (KJV) (Nelson, 2003) Joy is mostly composed of gratitude. Gratitude produces joy. Our gratitude should be for other people's blessings as well as for our own. When we take away resentment, anger, fear, worry, materialism, greed, jealousy, complaining and pride, the end result is Joy! Joy is a major topic in the Bible. It appears over 100 times in the King James Version of the Bible and rejoice appears approximately 198 times not counting other versions of the word such as joyful, joyfully, joyous, jubilant, happy and glad. Joy is not optional. The Bible commands us to rejoice. Paul says, "Rejoice in the Lord always. Again, I will say, rejoice!" Philippians 4:4 (NKJV) (Nelson, 2003) We have a reason to rejoice because it is the trials that help to build Godly character. "We know that all things work together for good to those who love God, to those who are the called according to His purpose." (Romans 8:28 KJV) (Nelson, 2003) James wrote, "My brethren, count it all joy when you fall into various trials, knowing that the testing of your faith produces patience." James 1:2-3 (NKJV) (Nelson, 2003) We can be filled with joy and the Holy Spirit as the disciples were according to Acts 13:52 (NKJV). God is joyful therefore His servants should be joyful. We should repent and be baptized in the name of Jesus Christ for forgiveness of our sins. When God comes into our lives, a unique joy begins to live within us.

 Peace

"Only God can create peace through the works of the Holy Spirit." (Ministries, 2002-2019) The Fruit of the Spirit includes a peace that goes beyond that of salvation." (Ministries, 2002-2019) There is the peace of God and peace with God. We have access to both. Romans 5:1 (NKJV) summarized; we have peace with God because we have been justified through faith. We have been declared righteous because of the atonement. Ephesians 2:14 (NKJV) states "For He Himself is our peace, who has made both one, and has broken down the middle wall of separation." Colossians 1:20 (NKJV) speaks of having made peace through the blood of His cross. When we are a part of His family, we should pray with confidence, knowing authority has been given to us. We have access to peace because of our faith. There is a heavenly account that has been purchased by God. Faith and the name of Jesus is the access code. "It's the prescription for receiving God's peace. The direction is twofold. Don't worry about anything and pray about everything in a spirit of thanksgiving and gratitude." (Larson, 1966 revised 1984, p. 537) "The Spirit filled Christian has a peace that is abundant, available in every situation unlike anything that the world has to offer." "Peace I leave with you, My peace I give to you; not as the world gives do I give to you. Let not your heart be troubled, neither let it be afraid." John 14:27 (KJV)

Patience

What does it mean to be patient? To be patient is "to be able to accept or tolerate delays, problems or suffering without becoming annoyed or anxious." The two Greek words translated as patience are Hupomonc which means "a remaining under" and Makrothumia, literally meaning long temper. Long temper is translated in the King James Version as long suffering. A patient person is able to endure much pain and suffering without complaining. A patient person knows how to wait on God for direction and for God to comfort and punish wrong doings. Patience brings self-restraint and careful thinking. Having patience is a sign of strength contrary to what many believe. Being impatient is actually a weakness. As God is patient with us, we should be patient with others. We should pray to have the patience of Christ. Romans 2:4 (KJV) states that the goodness of God leadeth thee to repentance. We should not despise the riches of His goodness, forbearance and longsuffering. The opposite of patience is agitation, discouragement and a desire for revenge. As the Bible teaches, we are not to avenge ourselves; rather, we are to love others. God is patient and His Spirit is the fruit of patience within us.

Dr. Tomeka Wooten

Gentleness

Gentleness embodies kindness and is more of a way of life. Kindness and gentleness are interrelated. Kindness and gentleness are fruits of the spirit. These characteristics are the results of anyone who allows the Holy Spirit to develop maturity in their lives. "Chrestotes is the Greek word for kindness. It means benignity, tender concern or uprightness." (Ministries, 2002-2019) On multiple occasions, kindness induced Jesus to stop what He was doing to help others in need. When we exhibit the kindness of God, we are tender, benevolent and useful to others. Sometimes it's hard to maintain this attitude towards people and the ones we love, especially our enemies. For this, it requires a work of God and thus is known as a fruit of the Spirit. We can't do it by our own power or strength, it by the Holy Spirit. It is kindness that led God to provide salvation for us. Gentleness is the quality of being kind and mild mannered.

Gentleness looks like kindness and sometimes it can be confused with weakness. Kind words and actions proceed from a pure heart. "By long forbearance a ruler is persuaded, And a gentle tongue breaks a bone." Proverbs 25:15 (NKJV) Kindness is a quality of being friendly and doing well to other people. Kindness speaks truth in love. Jesus was not nice but kind and gentle. He was the most perfect image of kindness and gentleness. "17 But the wisdom that is from above is first pure, then peaceable, gentle, willing to yield, full of mercy and good fruits, without partiality and without hypocrisy." James 3:17 (NKJV). 24 And a servant of the Lord must not quarrel but be gentle to all, able to teach, patient," 2 Timothy 2:24 (NKJV) (Nelson, 2003)

Goodness

The first place in the Old Testament where something is called good is Genesis 1. As God spoke into existence each phase of creation, He saw that it was good. What does this mean? How could it have been bad or evil? I believe the point here involves expected function. God's creation did what He intended it to do. It accomplished its purpose. It met His expectations and that is one of the basic ideas of the goodness the Spirit wants to manifest in our lives. Goodness is holiness in action, it is a virtue. It results in a life characterized by deeds motivated by righteousness and a desire to be a blessing. Goodness is a moral characteristic of a Spirit-filled person. "In the Greek, goodness translates to agathosune and is defined as uprightness of heart and life." (Ministries, 2002-2019)

"Agathosune is goodness for the benefit of others, not goodness simply for the sake of being virtuous. Someone with agathosune will selflessly act on behalf of others." (Ministries, 2002-2019)

Confronting someone about a sin demonstrates goodness. Expressions of goodness are as varied as the Spirit is creative. Goodness is not a quality we can manufacture on our own. James says, "Every good gift and every perfect gift is from above, and comes down from the Father of lights, with whom there is no variation or shadow of turning." James 1:17 (NKJV) (Nelson, 2003) This certainly includes a life characterized by goodness. In letting the Holy Spirit control us, we are blessed with the fruit of goodness. In the same way, "Let your light so shine before men, that they may see your good works and glorify your Father in heaven. (Matthew 5:16 (NKJV). Our hearts should match our actions. God is just as concerned about our heart as He is our actions. James wrote to the early Christians, instructing them to cleanse their hands (actions), you sinners; and purify your hearts (attitudes), you double-minded (straddling the fence between God and the world)." James 4:8 (Nelson, 2003) Pure hearts require right motives. Paul basically explains in 1 Corinthians 13:3 (NKJV) that if he did good works without love, "it profits him nothing." (Nelson, 2003)

Deeds such as giving to the poor, providing for one's children, visiting the sick, volunteering to clean up after a storm and praying for an enemy are all good deeds. However, doing good deeds to impress others will bring no reward from God. Summarized in Matthew 6:1-4 (KJV). But when the motive is to "glorify your Father in heaven" instead of yourself, doing good works that are seen by others is part of being "the light of the world" mentioned in Matthew 5:14-16 (KJV) (Nelson, 2003). Though our natural inclination is to defy God in sin, He has determined to help us overcome that nature to live a life of righteousness and goodness. This is possible only through a relationship with Him. As the Apostle John explained, "He who does good [as a way of life] is of God, but he who does evil [as a way of life] has not seen God [i.e., has not come to really know Him.]" 3 John 1:11 (NKJV) (Nelson, 2003) Good works include obeying God's laws. God gives His Holy

Spirit "to those who obey Him" according to Acts 5:32 (NKJV) (Nelson, 2003). That doesn't mean salvation can be earned by obedience. We are saved by God's grace, which "is the gift of God." Ephesians 2:8 (NKJV) (Nelson, 2003). However, we are being "created in Christ Jesus for good works." (Nelson, 2003) He who loves God will gladly demonstrate that love for God by keeping His commandments! It takes courage to obey God, because it often brings persecution: When you do good and suffer, if you take it patiently, God will greatly bless you, 1 Peter 2:20 (KJV) Compare Matthew 5:10 (KJV). Christ said to do good to everyone, even our enemies! "But I say to you who hear: Love your enemies, do good to those who hate you, bless those who curse you, and pray for those who spitefully use you." Luke 6:27-28 (NKJV) (Nelson, 2003) We cannot produce goodness on our own. Every good and perfect gift is from above. This certainly includes a life blessed with the fruit of goodness which comes when we let the Holy Spirit control us.

Faithfulness

Faithfulness is a fruit of the Spirit, it's the result of the Spirit working in us. But, the Spirit is also our seal of faithfulness. He is our witness to God's promise that if we accept the truth about God, He will save us. Faithfulness is believing that God is who He says He is, despite the vagaries of life. Functionally, that means we trust what God says in the Bible and not necessarily what the world or our own eyes tell us. We trust He will work out everything for good. We trust He will work His will in us and our situation on earth is nothing compared to our future reward in heaven. The only way we can have such faith is by the Holy Spirit's influence. He testifies to the truth and impels us to seek God. The Spirit makes us faithful. The fruit of the Spirit produces faith and confidence in a person's life. In the life of the believer, we are to live with inner peace and a total trust in God and His Way and Plan. Fear is to have no place in our lives. 2 Timothy 1:7 (NKJV) For God has not given us a spirit of fear, but of power and of love and of a sound mind." Fear has no place in our heart and mind.

God's standard of faith and faithfulness is far greater than what we can achieve with our own human effort. Although all people sometimes fail at faithfulness, we can always count on God. That is what enables us to have complete faith and trust in Him. It's vital that we respond to the faithfulness of God the Father and Jesus Christ with deep and abiding trust. It's only then that we are able to give our very best, our utmost allegiance, fidelity, obedience and devotion, produced through the Holy Spirit. In order to reach the level of faith to truly become pleasing to God, we must wholeheartedly seek His help by praying for faith, faithfulness, reading the Bible and trusting in Him. It will inspire us to follow His example just as His servants in times past. Seek the fellowship of "the church of God" where others are trying to faithfully follow Him today. Acts 2:42 (NKJV) states "And they continued steadfastly in the apostles' doctrine and fellowship, in breaking of bread, and in prayers." Summarized in 2 Timothy 1:13-14 (NKJV) "To truly "hold fast" spiritually, we must have God's Spirit dwelling within us. How do we obtain God's Spirit? Right after the Apostle Peter preached a powerful sermon, he told the listeners, "Repent, and let every one of you be baptized in the name of Jesus Christ for the remission [forgiveness] of sins; and you shall receive the gift of the Holy Spirit." Acts 2:38 (NKJV). God's Spirit then imparts the nature of God, which develops in us gradually, like fruit ripening on a tree. The "fruit" that God's Spirit produces is composed of many wonderful virtues.

 Meekness

Spiritual meekness is the antithesis of self-will, self-interest and self-assertiveness. It has been defined several ways: righteous, humble, teachable and patient under suffering. Long suffering with the willingness to follow gospel teachings is an attribute of a true disciple. To be meek is to have a mild temper. To be soft, gentle, not easily provoked or irritated, yielding and given to forbearance under injuries. According to Numbers 12:3 (NKJV), "(Now the man Moses was very humble, more than all men who were on the face of the earth.)" (Nelson, 2003) To be meek also means to continually practice humility in an evangelical sense. Submitting to God's divine will, not proud, not or refractory, not peevish or apt to complain about divine dispensations. Christ says, "Take my yoke upon you and learn from Me, for I am gentle and lowly in heart, and you will find rest for your souls." (Matt.11:29) (Nelson, 2003) Blessed are the meek, For they shall inherit the earth. (Matthew: 5:5 NIV) (Nelson, 2003)

Dr. Tomeka Wooten

Temperance

Temperance means self-control. It is control over the whole man (spirit, soul and body) which enables us to live a victorious life. "And everyone who competes for the prize is temperate in all things. Now they do it to obtain a perishable crown, but we for an imperishable crown." I Corinthians 9:25 (NKJV). A person who has self-control is mild, calm, avoids extreme behavior and exercises self-restraint in both actions and speech. Although restraint and self-control aren't easy, they are necessary if one ever wants to operate in the fruit of the Spirit. After all, temperance and love are the bookends that hold all the other fruit in place. The Bible tells us that our spirits and our flesh will war against each other in this life. Our flesh wants immediate self-gratification at all costs and will stop at nothing to try and get it. Our spirits know that some of our fleshly desires are not right for us, resulting in a major tug of war between the two. The only thing that will be able to control and curb some of the desires of our flesh is the quality of self-control. According to Webster's dictionary, the definition of temperance is "moderation in action, thought, or feeling restraint, habitual moderation in the indulgence of the appetites or passions, moderation in or abstinence from the use of alcoholic beverages." (Webster's dictionary) Temperance is a Gift from God and is something that must be practiced. Summarized in Romans 13:13-14 (NKJV) "There are the things to bring under Christ's control: our tongue, our thoughts, our temper (anger), our thirst, our passions and desires, our trades, our very life itself, what we do with it and even our tipple (alcohol). Ephesians 5:18 (NKJV) states "And do not be drunk with wine, in which is dissipation; but be filled with the Spirit." The Bible does not use the word self-control extensively. However, it is implied in many exhortations to obedience, submission and sinless living. Another Greek word, nephalios has the same general meaning. It generally covers a more specific area of self-control. It is often translated as "temperate" or "sober." Even though its root condemns self-indulgence in all forms, the Bible's writers use it to refer to avoid drunkenness. These words also include the notion of having complete clarity of mind, good sense and wisdom. All things being done in moderation and soundness of mind. It describes being watchful and remaining free from the intoxicating effects of the world, the flesh and Satan. The picture is that of a city whose walls have been nearly destroyed, rendering them defenseless against the enemy. So is the man who has no restraint over his spirit, the source of man's passionate energies. Proverbs shows a more positive side of self-control: "He who is slow to anger is better than the mighty, and he who rules his spirit than he who takes a city." Proverbs 16:32 (NKJV) (Nelson, 2003) Here Solomon uses an entirely different word for "rule," but the sense of self-control remains. A comparison of the two proverbs reveals the great importance of self-control as both an offensive and defensive attribute. Undoubtedly, self-denial, self-sacrifice and self-control are inextricably linked to a Christian life. Yet human nature exerts a persistent and sometimes very strong force away from God as Romans 8:7 (NKJV) clearly shows, "Because the carnal mind is enmity against God; for it is not subject to the law of God, nor indeed can be." (Nelson, 2003) It is this force that each Christian must overcome; controlling ourselves and denying human nature and its impulses to satisfy its desire. Sacrificing ourselves is necessary if we are to stop sinning as a way of life. When we add the concepts of self-denial and self-sacrifice to our understanding of self-control, we can see more clearly how large a role self-control plays in the Bible. The last fruit that Paul lists is self-control or temperance. A principle of interpretation we use when qualities like this are listed is that the most important comes first. However, why does Paul list them in this order? The list begins with "love" and ends with "self-control/temperance." Paul arranged this list in this order because it takes love to precipitate all the other characteristics and if a person truly walks in the Spirit, the fruit will culminate in temperance. Self-control is not the least of the fruit of the Spirit but a major goal. We do not sin because we are ignorant, but because we simply will not make the sacrifice to control ourselves. Were Adam and Eve in ignorance when they sinned? Of course not! They sinned because they did not control themselves to obey what they knew. If this principle were not so, God could not hold the uncalled, the spiritual Gentiles of this world, guilty based on natural law. Romans 2 (NKJV) makes it clear the uncalled know a great deal, but even with that knowledge, they still do not submit. Temperance is the fruit that when applied to life, provides the right balance to glorify God. Temperance, in modern English, usually refers only to restraint toward alcoholic beverages, but the biblical application is much broader. The Greek word, engkrateia, is the noun form of a verbal root that means "strong in a thing, strength, power, dominion, having power over, being master of." It is synonymous with "self-mastery" or "self-control." Paul uses it this way in relation to the general demeanor of a bishop in Titus 1:8 (NKJV): "But hospitable, a lover of what is good, sober-minded, just, holy, self-controlled." He applies it to sex in 1 Corinthians 7:9 (NKJV), "But if they cannot exercise self-control let them marry. For it is better to marry than to burn with passion." In 1 Corinthians 9:27 (NKJV), "But I discipline my body, and bring it into subjection, lest, when I have preached to others, I myself should become disqualified." This word describes his discipline of his body in following this way of life." The influences of the Holy Spirit on the heart make a man moderate in all indulgences; teaching him to restrain his passions and to govern himself; to control his evil propensities and to subdue all inordinate affection. A Christian must be a temperate man and if the effect of his religion does not produce this, it is false and vain. He that is under the influence of the Spirit of God is thoroughly a man of temperance. When we add the concepts of self-denial and self-sacrifice to our understanding of self-control, we can see more easily how large a role self-control plays in the church. Self-control is an attribute of our Creator. Jesus exemplified it in His life and Paul strongly exhorts us to exercise it in our life. If we are to be made in our Father's image, we will yield to God in this matter to glorify Him with our moderation in all things and rigid resistance to sin.

"The fruits of the Spirit therefore flow out of obedience." (Kendall, 1996, 1998, 1999, 2000, 2002, 2014, p. 195) We have to resist the flesh as well as hate the work of the flesh. Once we become open to the Spirit, we start to manifest these fruits of the Holy Spirit. They are the genuine marks of godliness. They are the virtues we see eminently and vividly modeled in the lives of mature Christians. They are the virtues our Lord wants us to cultivate. They are essential to the maturation of Christ in the Saints that they may be found ready and waiting upon his return. They are the virtues that are the gifts of God. God promises to reward these virtues in us. "These nine manifestations of The Fruit of The Holy Spirit will enable us to eliminate spiritual barrenness, escaping the corruption of the world and become partakers of the divine nature of God; growing spiritually and witnessing to unbelievers as well." (Fruit of the Holy Spirit, 1998) "True spirituality is the Fruit of the Spirit" (Kendall, 1996, 1998, 1999, 2000, 2002, 2014, p. 338) As Jesus said, "you will know them by their fruits." Matthew 7:16 (NKJV) (Nelson, 2003) God wants all of us to enter into a true sanctification process with Him so that He can begin a work in us. He wants to start the process of molding, shaping and transforming us into the image of His Son Jesus Christ. He wants to make us into a better and a holy people for His Glory! He wants to transform us by the renewing of our minds. He wants to put right thinking into our thought process and we have to be willing to work in cooperation with the Holy Spirit once He begins to start this sanctification process within us. "Abide in Me, and I in you. As the branch cannot bear fruit of itself, unless it abides in the vine, neither can you, unless you abide in Me. John 15:4 (NKJV) (Nelson, 2003) The fruit is not something that we have to work for, but what happens when we remain in the vine. The fruit is not the seed. The Holy Spirit is the seed in which that which produces the fruit. If we abide in the Lord, God our Father, stay connected and close, stay consistent with prayer and studying His word, the fruit will manifest in our lives. Each fruit derives out of love and is held together by self-control.

Seasons

To produce a good harvest the earth needs seasons. Just like nature has four different seasons, our lives seem to have different spiritual seasons. In earthly seasons, spring brings new beauty along with its showers. Summer brings warmth and sunshine along with its heat and thunderstorms. Fall brings coolness and colors along with its "falling away." Winter brings rest and peace along with its cold which may confine us. According to Ecclesiastes 3:1 (NKJV) "To everything there is a season, A time for every purpose under heaven."

Seasons are needed for growth, maturity, building, developing, sowing and reaping. Fall and winter are as contributive to our growth as spring and summer. Death and life are inseparable; they support each other. Something must die for something to live. God uses these times of seasons to strengthen us and rest. Seasons are created solutions for a right now problem. God knew that our seasons are attached to our assignments. It has everything to do with right timing.

Ecclesiastes 3:1-8 (NKJV) "To everything there is a season, And a time for every [a]purpose under heaven: 2 a time to be born, and a time to die; a time to plant, and a time to pluck what that is planted; 3 a time to kill, and a time to heal; a time to break down, and a time to build up; 4 a time to weep, and a time to laugh; a time to mourn, and a time to dance; 5 a time to cast away stones, and a time to gather stones together; a time to embrace, and a time to refrain from embracing; 6 a time to gain, and a time to lose; a time to keep, and a time to throw away; 7 a time to tear, and a time to sew; a time to keep silence, and a time to speak; 8 a time to love, and a time to hate; a time for war, and a time for peace." We may not always know the times or the seasons. And in Acts 1:7-8 states "And He said to them, "It is not for you to know times or seasons which the Father has put in His own authority. But you shall receive power when the Holy Spirit has come upon you; and you shall be witnesses to Me in Jerusalem, and in all Judea and Samaria, and to the end of the earth." 2 Timothy 4:1-8 (NKJV) "I charge you therefore before God and the Lord Jesus Christ, who will judge the living and the dead at His appearing and His kingdom: Preach the word! Be ready in season and out of season. Convince, rebuke, exhort, with all longsuffering and teaching. For the time will come when they will not endure sound doctrine, but according to their own desires, because they have itching ears, they will heap up for themselves teachers; and they will turn their ears away from the truth and be turned aside to fables. But you be watchful in all things, endure afflictions, do the work of an evangelist, fulfill your ministry.

Sometimes in life we may experience "dry" seasons, which could be times of disappointment, mistakes, grief or discouragement. Even if we are not facing huge trials, sometimes everyday activities can drain us dry. Heaven awaits those who put their faith and trust in Jesus Christ. He is the head of the faith which keeps us. Even in the darkest of seasons. Our fears tell us that we cannot manage this difficult season, in turn, we should give up. But as Galatians 6:9 (NKJV) states, "And let us not grow weary of doing good, for in due season we shall reap if we do not lose heart." But must remember not to give up, regardless of our situations. God has already made a way for us to return to the path He has set before us.

Proverbs 3:5-6 (NKJV) "Trust in the Lord with all your heart, And lean not on your own understanding; 6 In all your ways acknowledge Him, And He shall direct your paths." God sends seasons to give us rest so that we are refreshed. God uses seasons to help us grow in Him, and although He does not promise us a trial or rain-free life, He does promise to be with us in the storms! God may use these times of turbulent seasons or spiritual tribulation to strengthen us, but they also make us appreciate the calm seasons that much more! Seasons are imperative to yielding a good harvest. Human beings, like a farmer's crop, move through a growth process that culminates in a harvest of ripe produce. (Denee, n.d.)

Dr. Tomeka Wooten

The Former and Latter Rain

In agriculture there are a few specific stages involved in producing a good final harvest. The planting, the germination of the seed by the early rains, the maturation period and finally the ripening period brought on by the last rains of the season, called "the latter rain." The "latter rain" is biblically symbolic for the final outpouring of the Holy Spirit, by which the corporate spiritual church will be brought to ripeness for the harvest. Scriptures point toward a latter rain outpouring of God's spirit in the last days. "Blessed is the man whose strength is in You, Whose heart is set on pilgrimage. As they pass through the Valley of Baca, they make it a spring; the rain also covers it with pools" (Psalm 84:5-6, NKJV).

As we continue through the autumn season, I would like to turn your attention to the "autumn rains" mentioned in the psalm above. There are several references to autumn rains in the Bible. Depending on the Bible translation, sometimes you see autumn rain referred to as "early rain" or "former rain." The reason the Bible specifically mentions the rain of the autumn season is that such precipitation was very significant when the Bible was written. At that time, farmers in Israel would plant their crops in the autumn and then harvest them in the spring. Such practice revolved around the rain patterns of their climate. In the summer, there was very little to no rain. However, a rainy season would begin in autumn and then continue through winter and spring. Therefore, the autumn rains were extremely important, because they broke the summer drought and softened the parched land. Farmers depended on the rainfall to make planting possible. While the farming practices of our culture today may be different, we can still gain spiritual insight from Scriptures that refer to autumn rain.

Beyond the literal meaning of rain as precipitation, there is great symbolic significance to the autumn rains in the Bible. Just as rain refreshes dry soil, God refreshes the souls of His people with His Holy Spirit. Sometimes in life we may experience "dry" seasons, which could be times of disappointment, mistakes, grief, or discouragement. Even if we aren't facing huge trials, sometimes everyday activities can drain us dry. However, if we will keep our faith and confidence in Jesus, He will surely bring the "autumn rains" of His Spirit to encourage our hearts. We can find several keys to experiencing the rain of God's Spirit by looking again at Psalm 84:5-6 (NKJV) **The** psalmist writes, "Blessed is the man whose strength is in You, Whose heart is set on pilgrimage. As they pass through the Valley of Baca, they make it a spring; the rain also covers it with pools."

"Blessed are those whose strength is in you." This statement teaches us that we must find our strength in God alone. The psalmist continues, "… whose hearts are set on pilgrimage." A pilgrimage is a spiritual journey with a specific destination. Our journey should be a pursuit of God in which we dedicate our lives to fulfill His vision and plan.

The next phrase provides another key. "As they pass through the

Valley of Baca." The "Valley of Baca" can be translated as the "Valley of Weeping" and represents those dry seasons of life. You may have experienced some "Valleys of Weeping," and you may even be in such a valley right now. However, it's critical to note that the people who put their strength in God "pass through" the valley. When you experience valleys in life, God wants you to "pass through" them, not stay in them! Don't stop in the valley; keep following after God!

"And it shall be that if you earnestly obey My commandments which I command you today, to love the Lord your God and serve Him with all your heart and with all your soul, then I will give you the rain for your land in its season, the early and latter rain, that you may gather in your grain and your new wine and your oil. And I will send grass in your fields for your livestock, that you may eat and be filled, Deuteronomy 11:13-15 (NKJV). In Jeremiah 5:24 (NKJV) God declares that "They do not say in their heart, "Let us now fear the LORD our God, Who gives rain, both the former and the latter, in its season. He reserves for us the appointed weeks of the harvest."

This is a reminder that a lot of life is what you make it! We have the potential to take bad circumstances and "make" something good. As farmers look for rain to end their dry season, I encourage you to look for the "autumn rains" of God's Spirit. Place your strength in God, commit your heart to follow Him, keep going even in difficult times and choose to make something good of your situation. "Repent and turn to God … that times of refreshing may come from the Lord" (Acts 3:19). (Jackson, n.d.)

The Prophet and the Prostitute

In the book of Hosea, he was called to speak on God's behalf. Hosea experienced a broken marriage to Gomer in which she committed adultery. They had three children. God tells Hosea that despite Gomer's unfaithfulness, he is to go find her, pay off her debts to her lovers and once again commit his love and faithfulness to her. This story is symbolic of God's love for Israel. God entered into a covenant with Israel asking them to be faithful to Him alone. He brought them into the promised land and they dedicated all that God had given them to the worship of the Canaanite God; Baal. God could have ended the covenant divorcing Israel, but He did not. He decided to pursue Israel again and renew the covenant because of His love, compassion and faithfulness. Israel encountered severe consequences for their rebellion, but God's love and mercy outweighed their sin. As like today, God's desire is for us to have a personal relationship with Him. "Sow to yourselves in righteousness, reap in mercy; break up your fallow ground: for it is time to seek the Lord, till he come and rain righteousness upon you." Hosea 10:12 (KJV).

He wants us to know Him so that He can transform our hearts and in return we can show our love for Him. Israel was constantly breaking commandments. Hypocrisy, idol worshiping and trusting in political alliances instead of trusting in Him. This is the same thing that is going on in the world today. Ultimately, Hosea caused

Israel to repent and turn back to their God. God said that He would heal their waywardness and love them freely. This would require an act of God's grace and healing power to repair deep brokenness and sinful selfishness of the human heart so that His people could receive His love and love Him in return. His ultimate purpose is to heal and save His people according to Hosea 14:4-9 (KJV).

The Maturation of Christ in the Saints

Apostle Paul addressed the church at Corinth expressing the many problems that the early church faced. These are many of the same problems churches are facing today due to lack of knowledge, understanding and growth. As individuals we must grow and develop physically, mentally and spiritually. We must mature within the body of Christ (the church). The lambs must mature into sheep. It is time for babes to become mature members of the body. "As we so diligently prepare and educate ourselves in the things and ways of this world system, then even more so should we diligently pursue the things of God. As believers, we have an obligation to sharpen ourselves through the Word of God and knowledge of Christ; who is the head of the Body. We have an obligation to grow and function as true ambassadors of Christ. As we reach various stages of development in our spiritual growth, the main objective is to continue to grow." (https://theogolly.wordpress.com/2014/09/26/the-maturing-of-the-saints-i-cor-1311/, n.d.)

We have been called by Jesus to be fishers of men; to win souls. We have been equipped for the journey. The Saints should not be dismayed because we should be standing on the Word of God which is unchanging. Nothing should come by surprise. We should be encouraged through God's word to keep pressing towards the mark of the high calling, that we are able to endure. 2 Timothy 4:2

(NKJV), "Preach the word! Be ready in season and out of season. Convince, rebuke, exhort, with all long-suffering and teaching." This is the mark of excellence, the mark of a matured Saint. Maturation in Christ, always learning and being a student of the Word, gives God Glory!

Despite what some may believe, Christ will return, and our job is to always be ready. There is a sense of urgency of preparation. The latter rain is biblically symbolic for the final outpouring of the Holy Spirit, by which the corporate spiritual experience of God's church will be brought to ripeness for the harvest.

The Last Great Outpouring

Of the Holy Spirit

The Days of Joel 2 and Acts 2; The Sovereign Act of the Holy Spirit. "One last and final move of God upon the entire earth" " But this is that which was spoken by the prophet Joel; And it shall come to pass in the last days, saith God, I will pour out of my Spirit upon all flesh: and your sons and your daughters shall prophesy, and your young men shall see visions, and your old men shall dream dreams: And on my servants and on my handmaidens I will pour out in those days of my Spirit; and they shall prophesy: Acts 2:16-18 (KJV) When did the last days begin? According to Isaiah 2:1-2 (KJV) The word that Isaiah the son of Amoz saw concerning Judah and Jerusalem. 2 And it shall come to pass in the last days, that the mountain of the Lord's house shall be established in the top of the mountains and shall be exalted above the hills; and all nations shall flow unto it. Our question is when did the last days begin?

Isaiah wrote that when Israel and "more specifically Jerusalem" was re-established, this took place in June 1967. THEN this single event marks the beginning of "The Last Days"

Also wish to point out another word from the above verse. "I will pour out of my Spirit upon all flesh." Notice the word "all" is used. So this is a future event since at no time in history has God's Spirit fallen on ALL Flesh. The Spirit fell on the 120 in the upper room and countless believers since then but has never fallen upon

ALL flesh. Years ago, the Spirit revealed:

"The greater the intensity of the work, the shorter the time period." Man completes his work in the earth in 6,000 years. "The Lord created the earth in six days. Jesus worked Salvation on the cross for six hours. So we see when a work of God is being conducted, the intensity of that work will dictate the length of it. The greater the intensity of the work dictates the length of its time. The work of John the Baptist was very intense and lasted somewhere around three to three and a half years. The works of Jesus lasted about three and three and a half years. The work of the two witnesses will continue for three and a half years while the 144,000 witnesses will complete their work in three years. In all four of these examples, we see that the greater the intensity of the work, the shorter the time period. In each case, the ministry period was three and three and a half years in length. Seeing these examples, we can now extrapolate that the coming Harvest will also extend for approximately the same amount of time, three to four years in length." All things revolve around the timing of the Feasts of Israel.

Since we are in these last days and a tremendous Harvest is both anticipated and imminent, yet prior to this event, one final event remains before the Harvest can begin. The Lord will always visit His House first! For the time is come that judgment must begin at the house of God: 1 Peter 4:17a (KJV) "There is about to be a visitation to the house of God, For many it will be welcomed and to others it will feel like judgment!" What you receive will depend entirely upon where you are in your relationship with the Lord. If you are close and laboring to enter into His rest, it will be a season of great refreshing, but much more. It will also usher in healing, restoration and wholeness. Many of the laborers for this work will have been prepared since they came forth from their mother's wombs. They have undergone times of countless troubles; many will have lost family, friends, businesses, jobs, homes and every conceivable thing all due to their faith. Everything that gave them comfort or pleasure. To those who find themselves outside of this relationship with the Lord, they will still feel that same Spirit of the Lord. However, the Spirit will bring forth conviction, shame, sorrow and hopefully repentance. "This will be a Sovereign Act of My Spirit" sayeth the Lord. This Last Great Outpouring will be suddenly!

Just as in the upper-room, He will come to those who have waited patiently upon Him. When He comes, a holy boldness will be given to those who have hungered for Him; fear and dread will flee. Obedience and purity will begin to reign and rule in the hearts and minds of those who are truly His. Prayer will become our constant companion. Love will permeate everything we speak and everything we do, especially how we conduct ourselves. Your work will be orchestrated by the Spirit and you will see fruit when you minister. A newness of commitment and steadfastness in the Lord will become your shield. Complete strangers will see your light and will actively pursue you. They will feel His presence upon you and desire to be close to you. They will fall into your hands for Salvation and deliverance. You will be unable to hide your hope and joy! Many of the laborers of this end time harvest whom the Lord said were so few will have illnesses, diseases and frailties. Many are older and have come to think they are no longer of use to the Kingdom. Yet, they have been faithful with little and are about to be entrusted with more authority than they ever imagined. They are those who have experienced life and hardships. They have suffered and yet gained wisdom and discernment. They have shown their resolve and followed after the Lord. They have waited upon Him and now are about to have their strength renewed as the eagles. Dear Saints, though the years have brought you anguish and tears and loss, He will not be a debtor to any. He is a rewarder of those who have diligently sought Him. We are about to see things too valuable, too precious and too magnificent; those things the Prophets have desired to see. When this final great outpouring of the Spirit begins, you may awaken like any other morning only to find that you were visited in the darkest time of your night. Now your body has been healed and you have been delivered from those things that hindered you. A new season, a new day and a new anointing is about to come upon you. All of this will only draw you closer to the Wonderful One! The Holy Spirit will visit the household of God first, only then can the Harvest begin!" (http://jeremiah111.org/?page_id=6078)

Conclusion

In closing, God specializes in using imperfect people for His Glory. When we look at the Bible, we know that the Bible may have been written by imperfect people that were used mightily, but it was inspired by a perfect God that has always had a plan. There will be some things that we go through in life that we don't always understand. We must know that although we may not understand at the time, everything works together for the good of those that love Christ. God has always had a plan. He does not want any of His children to perish, but rather they be saved. The things that we go through are shaping and maturing us in Christ. God alone is sovereign and even in our imperfections, God is still perfect! God chooses who He pleases. He chose you, that you may be used to accomplish what He wants accomplished in the earth. It's not our capability, it's our availability. He is omnipotent, omniscience, omnipresent and He chose you; consider it an honor. He saw something in you. He equipped you to handle whatever is thrown your way. He gives beauty for ashes and strength despite adversity! He has equipped and qualified us Saints. We have been anointed and appointed. We have been justified by faith, that we have peace with God through our Lord and Savior, Jesus Christ. It is through faith that we believe and know that Jesus paid the price on Calvary for every sin. Know who you are and who you belong to. When you look at the Royal family, they have rules and protocol that royalty are expected to abide by. They already know that they have a secured heritage and a line of successors, and they know exactly who they are and the benefits of it. You do not have to tell them what to do and how to act. They know their birth right, their place, and their line of succession whether it be King, Queen, Prince, Princess, Duke, Duchess, Countess, Earl or Lady and so forth. When we look at our identity, meaning who God has called or is calling us to be, God has to purge us of some things. Offenses, sins known and unknown, transgressions, iniquities and issues must be purged so that we can rightfully walk circumspectly in our God given calling, authority and purpose that He has for our life! As the saying goes for each level comes a new devil but with God, by turning opposition into growth and opportunity, we go higher in Christ. We do not stress. We have peace in God therefore we relax. We understand that we will reap a good harvest and we patiently wait on the outpouring of the Holy Spirit. He is cleansing us and as He washes us, He forgets what we have done, and He hides His face from our sins. The day of cleansing and purification is upon us. A revival is God's promise to those who meet His conditions. How does revival come?

It comes when God's people humble themselves, pray, seek His face and turn from their wicked ways 2 Chronicles 7:14 (NKJV). A revival is what brings in an outpouring! Although an outpouring is up to God, the revival is up to us. God tells us to break up our fallow ground. While some wait for change to come, we should be preparing the soil of our hearts, seeking the Lord and planting seeds of revival until He rains down righteousness upon us. Hosea 10:12 (NKJV). Those seeds are for this and following generations. God has given us what we need. The real question is, "What are we doing to fulfill the Great Commission with the revival outpouring God has already given us?" Will He find us faithful when He comes? The Outpouring of the spirit on the day of Pentecost was the former rain. The outpouring of the spirit in these latter days is the latter rain. The main purpose of the outpouring of His spirit is to produce a harvest of souls. Be patient therefore, brethren, unto the coming of the Lord. Behold, the husbandman waiteth for the precious fruit of the earth, and hath long patience for it, until he receives the early and latter rain" James 5:7 (KJV).

The Lord is not slack concerning his promise, as some count slackness, but is longsuffering toward us, not willing that any should perish but that all should come to repentance. 2 Peter 3:9 (NKJV) And it shall come to pass, that whosoever shall call on the name of the Lord shall be saved. Acts 2:21 (NKJV) I do believe that God is giving more people a chance to repent that they may be saved. We are in the final countdown towards the return of Jesus. The latter rain is soon to come. Then we will experience end time harvest of souls, rapture of the church, seven-year period of the great tribulation, second coming of Jesus Christ, establishment of the millennial reign of Jesus Christ on Earth and ultimately the creation of a New Heaven and New Earth.

In the midst of this season of uncertainty and darkness; Christians we will rise. We are already a part of God's movement.

As men and women of God, we must remain encouraged and steadfast. Understanding that we are in a season of a spiritual paradigm shift and we must adapt. Our souls as well as others depend on us being in an unwavering position. We do not compromise the gospel, but we must be open to adapting to the changing of times. We are the forerunners and the trailblazers. All eyes are on us. How do we handle what we go through? God wants His people to know and hold on. Our life experiences should not be pushing us away from Christ but drawing us closer to Him; thus ultimately bringing us into the full maturation of Christ in us.

This message is to encourage the saints to reflect, repent, recommit and refocus on God. This must take place so that a refreshing, renewal, restoration, reformation, a fresh fire, fresh oil and a fresh anointing is poured out! Reformation will not bring forth the good fruit of righteousness unless it is connected with the revival of the Spirit. Revival and reformation are to do their appointed work and in doing this work they must blend. They go hand and hand. Time out for traditions. Time out for idols. God is a jealous God and He will consume them all with His consuming fire. Time out for forms of godliness lacking power thereof. Time out for disobedience and rebellion, which is too, that of witchcraft. God wants the church to get back to the basics. If you are ready for the outpouring, know that this outpouring can't take place without change! The final outpouring is for the renewal of the church that believers walk in Godliness which have not been witnessed since apostolic times. "18 Do not remember the former things, nor consider the things of old. 19 Behold, I will do a new thing, now it shall spring forth; shall you not know it? I will even make a road in the wilderness, and rivers in the desert. 20 The beast of the field will honour Me, the jackals and the ostriches, because I give waters in the wilderness, and rivers in the desert, to give drink to My people, My chosen. 21 This people I formed for Myself; they shall declare My praise." Isaiah 43:18-21 (NKJV)

Dr. Tomeka Wooten

About the Author

Dr. Tomeka L. Wooten is a proud wife, mother, daughter, sister and friend. Her profession: she is a registered nurse with a fulfilling and thriving nursing career. She earned a doctoral degree in Theology from Middle Georgia College of Theology. Her objective is to pursue a deeper understanding and closer relationship with the Father, His Kingdom and His people; that she may walk in her anointing and who He has called her to be. She desires to be who God has called her to be and speak only what He would have her to speak. In truth and in love, help bring godly correction turning people's hearts back to God by warning His people that repentance takes place preventing judgment. Happily married for twenty-two years with two handsome and intelligent sons; ages twenty-one and twenty-six. She is a grandmother of a two-year-old grandson.

She considers herself a trailblazer, trendsetter and visionary. She's not a licensed professional counselor but is an ambassador for Christ that offers Godly counsel. Through the help of the Holy Spirit, she's a servant that inspires, encourages, counsels and mentors. She has a passion for God's Word, His people and repentance of sins. Unapologetic, proud ambassador for Christ, with a prophetic anointing. Saved, sanctified, and filled with the Holy Spirit and has been forgiven; saved by grace, healed, restored, redeemed and delivered with a passion to share the Gospel with the lost that others are saved as well.

References

Cook, D. J. (2006). *Revelation Commentary*. Columbus, Ga.: Brentwood Christian Press. *https://www.blueletterbible.org/study/larkin/dt/22.cfm*. (2018). Retrieved from https://www.blueletterbible.org.

Nelson, T. (1982). Retrieved from https://www.biblegateway.com/.

Treybig, D. (2018). Retrieved from https://lifehopeandtruth.com/prophecy/revelation/seven-churches-of-revelation/

Walvoord, J. (1989). The Revelation of Jesus Christ. In J. Walvoord, *Bible* (pp. 51-52).

Fruit of the Holy Spirit. (1998, May). Retrieved from https://www.christcenteredmall.com/teachings/fruits/index.htm

Graham, B. (2011, October 28). The Fruit of the Spirit. Retrieved from http://billygraham.org Kendall, R. (1996, 1998, 1999, 2000, 2002, 2014). Understanding Theology Volume I.

London: Christian Focus Publications, Geanies House, Fearn, Ross-shire, IV201TW, Great Brittian.

Larson, M. F. (1966 revised 1984). The New Unger's Bible Handbook. Chicago: Moody Press, The Moody Bible Institute of Chicago.

Last Name, F. M. (Year). Article Title. Journal Title, Pages From - To.

Last Name, F. M. (Year). Book Title. City Name: Publisher Name.

Ministries, G. Q. (2002-2019). Got Questions.org. Retrieved from http://www.gotquestions.net Nelson, T. (2003). The Holy Bible Old and New Testaments Authorized King James Version. Nashville: Thomas Nelson, Inc.

Dr. Tomeka Wooten

129